United States
Department of
Agriculture

Forest
Service

North Central
Research Station

**General Technical
Report NC-263**

LANDIS 4.0 Users Guide

LANDIS: A Spatially Explicit Model of Forest Landscape Disturbance, Management, and Succession

Hong S. He, Wei Li, Brian R. Sturtevant, Jian Yang, Bo Z. Shang, Eric J. Gustafson, and David J. Mladenoff

MISSION STATEMENT

We believe the good life has its roots in clean air, sparkling water, rich soil, healthy economies and a diverse living landscape. Maintaining the good life for generations to come begins with everyday choices about natural resources. The North Central Research Station provides the knowledge and the tools to help people make informed choices. That's how the science we do enhances the quality of people's lives.

For further information, contact:

North Central Research Station
USDA Forest Service
1992 Folwell Avenue
St. Paul, MN 55108

Or visit our web site:
www.ncrs.fs.fed.us

He, Hong S.; Li, Wei; Sturtevant, Brian R.; Yang, Jian; Shang, Bo Z.; Gustafson, Eric J.; Mladenoff, David J. 2005. LANDIS 4.0 users guide. LANDIS: a spatially explicit model of forest landscape disturbance, management, and succession. Gen. Tech. Rep. NC-263. St. Paul, MN: U.S. Department of Agriculture, Forest Service, North Central Research Station. 93 p.

LANDIS 4.0 is new-generation software that simulates forest landscape change over large spatial and temporal scales. It is used to explore how disturbances, succession, and management interact to determine forest composition and pattern. Also describes software architecture, model assumptions and provides detailed instructions on the use of the model.

KEY WORDS: Simulation model, landscape ecology, software documentation, decision support, forest management, manual.

The U.S. Department of Agriculture (USDA) prohibits discrimination in all its programs and activities on the basis of race, color, national origin, sex, religion, age, disability, political beliefs, sexual orientation, and marital or family status. (Not all prohibited bases apply to all programs.) Persons with disabilities who require alternative means for communication of program information (Braille, large print, audiotape, etc.) should contact USDA's TARGET Center at 202-720-2600 (voice and TDD). To file a complaint of discrimination, write USDA, Director, Office of Civil Rights, Room 326-W, Whitten Building, 1400 Independence Avenue SW, Washington, DC 20250-9410 or call 202-720-5964 (voice and TDD). USDA is an equal opportunity provider and employer.

ABOUT THE AUTHORS

Hong S. He
Assistant Professor
School of Natural Resources
University of Missouri
Columbia, MO

Wei Li
Computer Programmer
School of Natural Resources
University of Missouri
Columbia, MO

Brian R. Sturtevant
Research Ecologist
North Central Research Station
Rhinelander, WI

Jian Yang
PhD student
School of Natural Resources
University of Missouri
Columbia, MO

Bo Z. Shang
Post-doctoral Associate
School of Natural Resources
University of Missouri
Columbia, MO

Eric J. Gustafson
Research Ecologist
North Central Research Station
Rhinelander, WI

David J. Mladenoff
Professor
Department of Forest Ecology and Management
University of Wisconsin-Madison
Madison, WI

LANDIS 4.0 Dynamic Design
Hong S. He (1)

LANDIS 4.0 Overall Programming
Wei Li (1)

LANDIS 4.0 Succession/Dispersal Module
Design: David J. Mladenoff (2), Hong S. He (1)
Implementation: Hong S. He (1)

LANDIS 4.0 Fire Module
Design: Jian Yang (1), Hong S. He (1), Eric Gustafson (3)
Implementation: Jian Yang (1)

LANDIS 4.0 Wind Module
Design: David J. Mladenoff (2), Hong S. He (1)
Implementation: Hong S. He (1)

LANDIS 4.0 Harvest Module
Design: Eric J. Gustafson (3), Kevin K. Nimerfro (3), Stephen R. Shifley (3),
   David J. Mladenoff (2), Hong S. He (2), Patrick A. Zollner (3)
Implementation: Kevin K. Nimerfro (3)

LANDIS 4.0 Fuel Module
Design: Hong S. He (1), Bo Z. Shang (1), Thomas R. Crow (3),
   Eric J. Gustafson (3), Stephen R. Shifley (3)
Implementation: Bo Z. Shang (1)

LANDIS 4.0 Biological Disturbance Module
Design: Brian R. Sturtevant (3), Eric J. Gustafson (3), Wei Li (1),
   Hong S. He (1)
Implementation: Wei Li (1)

LANDIS 4.0 Input and Output Interface
Design: Hong S. He (1)
Implementation: Shihua Sun (1)

Institutions of the above individuals when they made contributions to LANDIS 4.0
   1. University of Missouri-Columbia
   2. University of Wisconsin-Madison
   3. USDA Forest Service North Central Research Station

Funding Support for LANDIS 4.0 Development
USDA FS North Central Research Station (90%)
University of Missouri GIS Mission Enhancement Program (10%)

The following individuals also made contributions to LANDIS 4.0 development:
Pat Zollner (USDA FS North Central Research Station), Robert Cummings
(USDA FS North Central Research Station), Robert Scheller (University of
Wisconsin-Madison), David Lytle (USDA FS North Central Research Station).

Contact
Dr. Hong S. He
School of Natural Resources, University of Missouri-Columbia, 203 ABNR
Building, Columbia, MO 65211
heh@missouri.edu

TABLE OF CONTENTS

1. WHAT IS THE LANDIS MODEL?

LANDIS is a spatially explicit landscape model designed to simulate forest landscape change over large spatial and temporal scales (Mladenoff *et al.* 1996, Mladenoff and He 1999). LANDIS 4.0 simulates the dynamics of forest succession, seed dispersal, wind, fire, biological disturbance (insects and diseases), harvesting, fuel accumulation and decomposition, and fuel management. Differing from most landscape models, LANDIS simulates multiple landscape processes in combination with the simulation of succession dynamics at the tree species level.

2. LANDIS MODEL DESIGN CONSIDERATIONS

LANDIS is designed with these considerations:

- It simulates forest landscape change over large spatial (103-107 ha) and temporal (101-103 years) scales with flexible resolutions (10-500 m pixel size), balancing ecological complexity with current and foreseeable computational capability.

- It simulates the main natural and anthropogenic disturbances and their interactions with adequate mechanistic realism for these broad scales.

- It simulates species-level forest succession in combination with disturbances and management.

- It assumes that detailed, individual tree information and within-stand processes can be simplified, allowing large-scale questions about spatial pattern, species distribution, and disturbances to be adequately addressed.

- It uses a component-based, object-oriented design that provides users with the flexibility of parameterizing and simulating only the processes of interest.

- It uses classified satellite imagery as input, and output is compatible with most GIS software.

- It requires moderate parameter input since, for most landscapes in these scale ranges, available input data may be coarse and parameters may be poorly estimated.

LANDIS does not predict specific disturbance or management events. Rather, it is a scenario model that compares long-term effects of various disturbance and management scenarios on the simulated landscape.

3. LANDIS IS SUITED TO ANSWER THE FOLLOWING QUESTIONS

- How do disturbance and successional dynamics interact to change forest patterns on large, heterogeneous landscapes and what are the expected recovery paths of the tree species after disturbance in the simulated landscape?

- Will fire suppression lead to large catastrophic fires? If a large catastrophic fire were to occur, what are the long-term effects on forested ecosystems?

- Where are areas of high fire probability and high potential fire intensity on forest landscapes? How do these areas change over time under different fuel reduction plans?

- What are the effects of common fuel treatments such as prescribed burning and coarse woody debris reduction? What should be the treatment frequency, size, and intensity in order to maintain a forested landscape where fire is less likely to occur?

- What are the effects of forest harvesting and do the harvest activities performed at the stand scale alter species composition and spatial pattern at the landscape scale?

- How does seed dispersal influence landscape change and how significant is the initial seed source abundance and distribution for ecological restoration?

- How does insect disturbance influence the spatio-temporal pattern of forest composition and age? Does insect damage significantly influence long-term likelihood of fire?

4.   LANDIS 4.0 RELEASE NOTE

LANDIS 4.0 is a computer program that simulates forest landscape change over large spatial (103-107 ha) and temporal (101-103 years) scales. It is a new generation program based on earlier versions of LANDIS (Mladenoff *et al.* 1996, Mladenoff and He 1999). LANDIS 4.0 uses a component-based approach to software design, which breaks the monolithic program into multiple small, stand-alone, and functionally more specific components. In LANDIS 4.0, each component (module) simulates a particular process and collectively they simulate forest landscape change under natural and anthropogenic disturbances.

The current version (LANDIS 4.0) has gone through considerable testing. However, it is possible that users will discover bugs that arise under conditions we did not test. Please report all bugs to Dr. Hong S. He, heh@missouri.edu. We anticipate correcting bugs periodically within the same revision with higher decimal version numbers (e.g., LANDIS 4.0.1). Substantial changes to the software, primarily associated with the addition of new features (e.g., new modules), will be released as a new version number (e.g., LANDIS 4.1). All changes associated with each release will be documented in the release notes.

5.   THE NEW FEATURES IN LANDIS 4.0

- LANDIS 4.0 is a component-based program using multiple dynamically linked libraries (DLLs), each having a standard interface and simulating a distinct process.

- A biological disturbance agent (BDA) module was added to LANDIS 4.0 to simulate the effects of one or more insect and/or disease disturbances.

- A fuel module was added to track fine fuel, coarse fuel, and live fuel and to evaluate the effects of common fuel treatments on the simulated fire risk (see section 9.5.7.6 for definition).

- LANDIS 4.0 has a newly designed fire module that incorporates terrain, wind, and fuel information into the simulation of fire.

- In LANDIS 4.0, landscape heterogeneity is no longer assumed to be stratified only by land type map (or ecoregion). Landscape heterogeneity can now be processed using individual disturbance regime maps as well as the land type map.

- LANDIS 4.0 is now a Windows program, with companion graphical interfaces for input (LI.exe) and viewing output (LV.exe), which are independent of GIS software.
- LANDIS 4.0 automatically detects and accepts 16-bit input for all input maps. Consequently, the number of map classes that can be processed has increased from 256 to 65,536.
- LANDIS 4.0 preserves all the functionality of previous versions of LANDIS (e.g., LANDIS 3.7).

6. LANDIS 4.0 DISCLAIMER

This software is in the public domain and is the intellectual property of the acknowledged individuals (see acknowledgments). The recipient may not assert any proprietary rights thereto nor represent it to anyone as other than a program of the University of Missouri-Columbia. LANDIS is provided without warranty of any kind. The user assumes all responsibility for the accuracy and suitability of this program for his/her application. In no event will the authors or the university be liable for any damages, including lost profits, lost savings, or other incidental or consequential damages arising from the use of or the inability to use this program.

The computer program described in this publication is available on request with the understanding that the U.S. Department of Agriculture cannot assure its accuracy, completeness, reliability, or suitability for any other purpose than that reported.

7. LANDIS 4.0 COPYRIGHT

LANDIS 4.0 was developed in the GIS and Spatial Analysis Laboratory at the University of Missouri-Columbia in collaboration with the USDA Forest Service, North Central Research Station. It is the intellectual property of the acknowledged individuals. The copyright is held by the University of Missouri-Columbia. LANDIS 4.0 is available free of charge by contacting Dr. Hong S. He, heh@missouri.edu, or by registering at the LANDIS 4.0 Web site (www.snr.missouri.edu/LANDIS).

8. HOW TO USE THIS GUIDE

This guide contains the necessary information and step-by-step instructions on how to prepare data for a LANDIS run. It also presents conventions for data organization and file naming. Most of the file formats are shown using examples. We suggest reading Chapter 9 completely before conducting a run. This guide provides a full description of all LANDIS parameters. However, since LANDIS is a fully modularized program, users need to parameterize only the succession module and the modules needed for their specific simulations. Users may find the troubleshooting tips helpful when doing their own runs. Please note that some recommendations from this chapter are from the developers' experience with only limited tests. We encourage users to read the publications on LANDIS for more technical issues. Also, please feel free to e-mail suggestions for expansions, limitations, or solutions to technical problems to the address on the bottom of page ii.

9.   CONCEPTUAL BASIS FOR THE LANDIS MODEL

9.1   Spatial and Temporal Scales of LANDIS

LANDIS is a spatially explicit landscape model designed to simulate forest landscape change over large spatial and temporal scales (Mladenoff *et al.* 1996, Mladenoff and He 1999). LANDIS 4.0 simulates the dynamics of forest succession, seed dispersal, wind, fire, biological disturbance (insects and diseases), harvesting, fuel accumulation and decomposition, and fuel management. Differing from most landscape models, LANDIS simulates multiple landscape processes in combination with the simulation of succession dynamics at the tree species level.

In LANDIS, a landscape is modeled as a grid of cells (or sites) with vegetation information stored as attributes for each cell (fig. 1). At each cell, the model tracks a matrix containing a list of species by rows and the 10-year age cohorts by columns. The temporal scales of LANDIS are largely dictated by the current 10-year age-cohort structure, and the 10-year time step makes the model suitable for simulating long-term dynamics (101-103 years). The spatial scales of LANDIS are between 103 and 107 ha, depending on the simulation cell size. Since LANDIS tracks only the presence/absence of species age cohorts, not individual trees, computational loads are greatly reduced. In addition, the essential information of presence/absence is relatively independent of cell size, and therefore LANDIS is capable of simulating forest succession at cell sizes ranging from 10 to 500 m (He *et al.* 1999a).

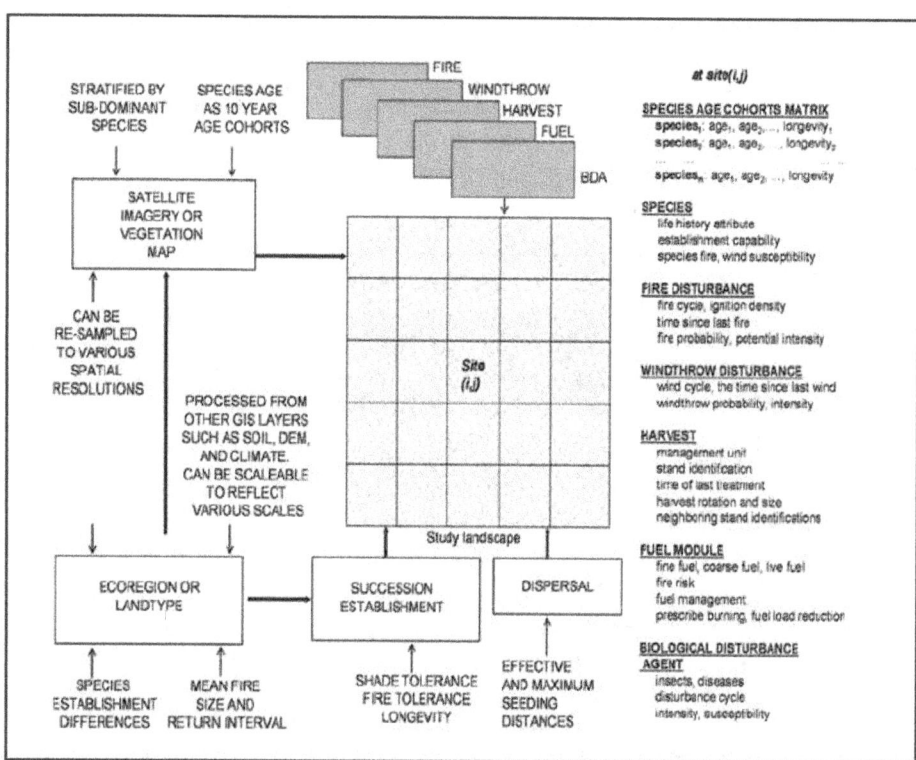

Figure 1. LANDIS model structure. In LANDIS, a landscape is divided into equal-sized individual cells or sites. Each site (i, j) resides on a certain land type and a disturbance regime type, and includes a unique list of species present and their associated age cohorts. The species/age cohort information varies with establishment, succession, and seed dispersal, and interacts with disturbances.

9.2 Heterogeneity

In LANDIS, heterogeneity of vegetation, disturbance, and management activities is modeled at multiple hierarchical levels from the landscape to the pixel. For vegetation heterogeneity, LANDIS stratifies the heterogeneous landscape into land types (also called ecoregions for broad-scale studies), which are generated from GIS layers of climate, soil, or terrain attributes (slope, aspect, and landscape position). Land types capture the highest level (coarse grain) of spatial heterogeneity caused by various environmental controls. Within a land type, a somewhat uniform suite of ecological conditions that results in similar species establishment patterns is assumed, but the stochastic processes such as seed dispersal can result in intermediate level (fine grain, within land type) heterogeneity of a species distribution. Finally, succession, competition, and probabilistic establishment may result in heterogeneity of species presence and age cohorts even among pixels that were initially identical. Disturbance heterogeneity refers to various regimes a disturbance may have on the simulated landscape. For disturbance heterogeneity (except for wind and biological disturbances), LANDIS stratifies the heterogeneous disturbance regimes using disturbance regime maps (fig. 1). For example, fire regimes are characterized by ignition frequency and fire cycle (mean fire return interval) in the fire regime map (Yang *et al.* 2004). Within-regime heterogeneity is further simulated by the stochastic process of each disturbance regime, and pixel level heterogeneity is simulated through the interaction of disturbance and the vegetation in the particular pixel. Furthermore, land types or disturbance regimes can be defined by users to partition the landscape into strata that are most relevant for a particular application.

9.3 Stochasticity

LANDIS is a stochastic model that uses random number generators to simulate the stochastic processes of seed dispersal, seedling establishment, disturbance, and management events. Therefore, LANDIS predicts the statistical properties of landscape composition, age structure, and spatial pattern under particular disturbance and management regimes, but it does not accurately predict individual disturbance events or optimize management actions.

9.4 Component-based Model Design

LANDIS 4.0 is a new generation program based on earlier versions of LANDIS (Mladenoff and He 1999). LANDIS 4.0 uses a component-based approach to conduct simulation, which breaks the monolithic program into multiple small, stand-alone, and functionally more specific components (He *et al.* 2002).

A component in a model is like a mini-model; it comes packaged as a binary code that is compiled, linked, and ready to perform certain tasks for the entire model. Components connect with each other at run time to form a complete model. With a component-based model, it is possible to replace some components while maintaining the integrity of the model. In LANDIS 4.0, each component (module) simulates a particular process and collectively they simulate forest landscape change under natural and anthropogenic disturbances (fig. 2).

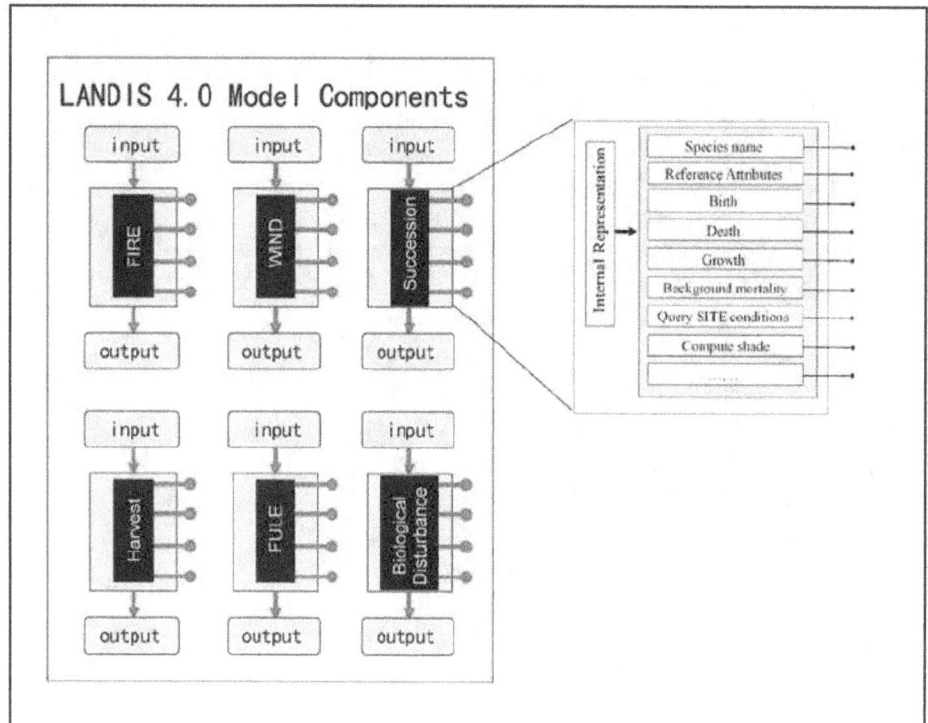

Figure 2. LANDIS 4.0 uses a component-based modeling approach. A component is like a mini-model with a published interface that can be updated or replaced by any group (Li and He 2004).

Breaking up a single monolithic program into several logically independent modules has the following advantages (He *et al.* 2002): 1) modifying and testing a component is a much smaller task than tackling a whole model; 2) keeping the logic of an ecological process contained within a single module ensures that changes to a module will not have unintended effects in other parts of the model; 3) components can be developed by different groups or in other programming languages; 4) upgrading the model is easier because existing components can easily be replaced by new components. This reduces the number of largely redundant versions of the model and allows the modeling community to focus on significant conceptual advances rather than managing cumbersome code. These advantages truly allow more groups to participate in the modeling work. For example, a disturbance may have several designs and implementations from different groups in the dynamically linked libraries format, which can be plugged into LANDIS 4.0 and run without recoding and recompiling the whole model. This provides an ideal platform for scientists to compare and analyze different disturbance module designs. Therefore, a component-based model can be more rigorously tested, evaluated, and modified than a monolithic model, and these processes can be conducted not only by the original developers, but by the larger modeling community (He *et al.* 2002).

9.5 Overview of LANDIS Model Components

9.5.1 Succession and Seed Dispersal

Succession is a non-spatial, site level process. In LANDIS, it is assumed that detailed, individual tree information and within-stand processes can be simplified, allowing large-scale questions such as spatial pattern, species distribution, and disturbances to be adequately addressed. Succession at each site is a competitive process driven by species life history attributes. These are longevity, age of sexual maturity, shade tolerance class, fire tolerance class, maximum age of vegetative reproduction (sprouting), sprouting probability, and effective and maximum seeding distance based on 10-year time step. In contrast to most gap models, which track individual trees (Botkin *et al.* 1972; Botkin 1993; Pastor and Post 1985; Shugart 1984, 1997; Urban *et al.* 1993), LANDIS tracks the presence and absence of species age cohorts. Therefore, succession dynamics is simplified and simulated as birth, growth, and death processes acting on species age cohorts. This approach is similar to a polygon-based landscape model, LANDSIM (Roberts 1996). During a single LANDIS iteration, birth, death, and growth routines are performed on species age cohorts and random background mortality is simulated.

9.5.1.1 *Birth, establishment, growth, and death*

In succession, several parameters are treated as categorical inputs rather than modeled explicitly; these include species shade tolerance class and fire tolerance class. Other parameters are treated as numerical inputs, including a species' effective and maximum dispersal distance.

Birth adds the presence of the youngest age cohort (1-10) to a species. When seed dispersal is simulated for a given site, a uniform random number from 0 to 1 is drawn to check against an establishment coefficient to decide if seed can establish. A species establishment coefficient is a number ranging from 0 to 1 that expresses the species' relative ability to grow on different site categories or land types. Coefficients are differentiated based on relative responses of species to soil moisture, climate, and nutrients and are not themselves modeled within LANDIS. They can be estimated empirically or derived from a gap model with ecosystem-process drivers (He *et al.* 1999b). A species can establish only when its establishment coefficient is greater than the random number drawn. Therefore, species with high establishment coefficients have a higher probability of establishment.

Growth increases all species age cohorts by 10 years, and death deterministically removes the species age cohort when it reaches the longevity of the species. Random background mortality simulates tree mortality as it approaches its longevity, but not the mortality caused by disturbance and harvest.

9.5.1.2 *Vegetative reproduction*

Vegetative reproduction may occur following the death of a species age cohort. The process of vegetative reproduction is simulated stochastically based on the species' sprouting probability. Maximum sprouting age is used to determine the age at which species can re-sprout in this version of LANDIS. When checking for the sprouting of a species on a given site, a uniform random number from 0 to 1 is drawn to check against the species' sprouting probability to decide if the species can reproduce vegetatively.

9.5.1.3 *Competition*

A species' competitive ability is determined based upon simple logical rules applied to the combination of life history attributes and land type suitability (Mladenoff and He 1999). Shade-intolerant species (species with lower shade-tolerance class) cannot establish either by seeding or by vegetative reproduction on a site where more shade tolerant and mature species are present. On the other hand, the most shade-tolerant species are delayed in being able to occupy an open site until the specified number of years of shade presence has passed. A shade-checking algorithm defines shade by the most shade-tolerant species cohort present that is also sexually mature. Species cohorts younger than the minimum seed-producing age are ignored in this shade-checking algorithm. This was implemented as a surrogate for crown closure. Without disturbance, shade-tolerant species will tend to dominate the landscape if other attributes are not highly limiting and land types (reflected as species establishment coefficients) are generally suitable.

9.5.1.4 Seed dispersal

Seed dispersal is modeled as a function of species effective and maximum seeding distances. The effective seed-dispersal distance is the distance at which seed has the highest probability (e.g., $P>0.95$) of reaching a site. The maximum seed-dispersal distance is that distance beyond which a seed has near zero probability (e.g., $P<0.001$) of reaching. These distances have been parameterized for common tree species in northern Wisconsin (Mladenoff and He 1999b) based on the literature for various tree species. Seed-dispersal probability (P) between the effective (ED) and maximum seeding distance (MD) follows a negative exponential distribution:

$$P = e^{-b \cdot (\frac{x}{MD})} \qquad (1)$$

where x is a given distance from the seed source (MD>x>ED), m is the maximum seeding distance, and b is an adjustable coefficient ($b>0$) ($b=1$ in the current version of LANDIS), which can change the shape of the exponential curve corresponding to various seed-dispersal patterns when information is available (fig. 3). If $x \leq$ ED, $P=0.95$, indicating that the probability of seed dispersing within its own effective seeding distance is very high, while if $x \geq$ MD, $P=0.001$, indicating that the probability of seed dispersing beyond its own maximum seeding distance is very low (He and Mladenoff 1999b).

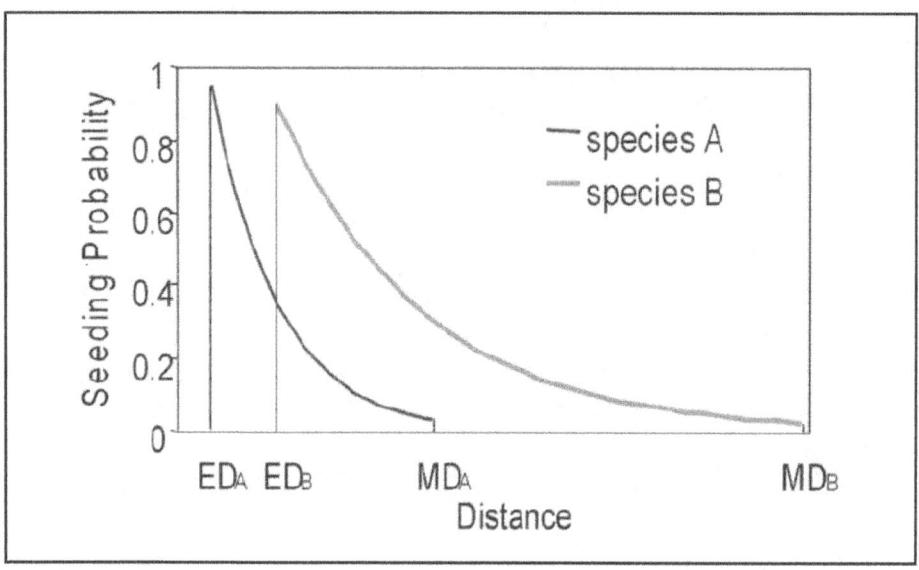

Figure 3. The negative exponential distribution of tree species seeding probability in relation to distance from available seed sources. ED—species effective seeding distance, MD—species maximum seeding distance. Other functions can also be used.

Other types of seed dispersal that are implemented include no dispersal (no cell receives seed), uniform dispersal (all cells receive seed from all species), and neighboring dispersal (seed only disperse to the neighboring cell).

9.5.2 Natural Disturbance Overview and Definitions

The ability to simulate different types of disturbances and management and their effects on tree communities and landscape structure is central to the design and intent of LANDIS. LANDIS 4.0 can simulate three different types of natural disturbances (fire, wind, and biological), implemented as independent modules that can be applied in any combination. While each disturbance module follows its own set of "rules" that define its spatiotemporal dynamics and impacts on simulated vegetation, some organizing themes are common to all disturbance modules described in this section. Several terms used to define the LANDIS disturbance rules have ambiguous definitions in the disturbance ecology literature, and some terms with slightly different meanings have been used interchangeably in different publications describing various LANDIS components. We attempt to reconcile these inconsistencies here by clearly defining key LANDIS disturbance terms to be most consistent with the literature. At times these definitions will conflict with past LANDIS publications; these discrepancies are noted within each individual module description.

Disturbance dynamics can be simplified into three steps: 1) selecting individual sites to be disturbed; 2) calculating disturbance intensity; and 3) removing susceptible and intolerant species-age cohorts (i.e., disturbance-caused mortality or effects). Disturbance site selection is a spatial process specific to each disturbance type. For example, a wind or fire event spreads across a subset of sites forming disturbance patches; a biological disturbance (e.g., insect) selects sites for disturbance using species and age composition; the harvest module selects group of sites (e.g., a stand) for a given treatment. In each case, the frequency and number of sites (i.e., area) disturbed by each disturbance module is controlled by user-defined but stochastic disturbance regimes.

Once a site is selected for disturbance, a disturbance *intensity class* is calculated based on a set of rules. Sousa (1984, page 357) defines disturbance intensity as "a measure of strength of the disturbing force." Examples include fire temperature, wind speed, or population size of defoliating insects. Intensity classes within LANDIS approximate the relative strength of the simulated disturbance event, and their specific calculation varies by disturbance module. Vulnerability to a given disturbance type can vary by both species and age. In LANDIS, *tolerance class* defines the relative vulnerability of a species to a given disturbance type and intensity, and *susceptibility class* defines the relative vulnerability of a species-age group to a given disturbance type and intensity (He and Mladenoff 1999). For example, fire is simulated, in general, as a bottom-up disturbance, in which the youngest age cohorts are most susceptible to mortality. However, a low intensity fire may not kill species of high fire tolerance class even if the age cohorts are young. Disturbance severity results from the interaction of disturbance intensity and species tolerance and susceptibility at each site, and it is calculated for each species age cohort present on that site to determine which species age cohorts are removed by the disturbance. Fire and BDA modules require both species tolerance and susceptibility classes to be defined, whereas the wind module does not require species tolerance classes, assuming that all species have similar vulnerability to wind disturbance.

Previous publications describing LANDIS fire (He and Mladenoff 1999) or biological disturbances (Sturtevant *et al.* 2004) used the term *severity class* to describe intensity class. However, severity is best defined as "the measure of damage caused by the disturbing force" (Sousa 1984, page 357), i.e., disturbance effects. He *et al.* (2004) and Shang *et al.* (2004) use the two terms interchangeably. Since actual disturbance effects in the form of species cohort mortality are implemented in a subsequent step, we use the term intensity class in the remainder of this users guide to represent the relative strength of a disturbance.

9.5.3 Fire Disturbance

Fire disturbance is an important landscape process. Fires appear to be stochastic for a single site, but have repeated patterns in terms of ignition, location, size, and shape at landscape scales. It has long been noted that some areas are more fire-prone than others. The differences are often represented by using mean fire-return interval, which is the mean number of years for fire to recur on a given area (Johnson 1992, Johnson *et al.* 1990, Pickett and Thompson 1978, Pickett and White 1985, Pickett *et al.* 1989). Depending on their extent, large landscapes can be stratified into ecoregions, relatively homogeneous sub-areas that are characterized by different climate, topography, and soils with similar fire characteristics. Such ecoregions can be used as the fire regime map in LANDIS in which each fire regime unit is characterized by its attributes in the fire regime attribute file.

As a disturbance module, a fire disturbance simulation module in LANDIS must address when and where such a disturbance occurs, how such a disturbance spreads over the landscape, and what effects it has on the forest landscape. Therefore, a fire module must include the following three major components:

- Fire occurrence simulates how many fires occur and when and where each fire occurs.

- Fire spread simulates how fires spread across the landscape from their ignition points.

- Fire effects simulates which species age cohorts are killed on each burned cell; the effects are quantified as fire intensity classes that are passed to the fuel module to determine how much fuel is consumed.

The fire module also reads its own input and writes its own output, just as the other modules do.

9.5.3.1 Fire occurrence simulation

The fire module in LANDIS 4.0 uses a hierarchical fire frequency model to simulate temporal patterns of fire regimes. This differs from past approaches (Baker *et al.* 1991, He and Mladenoff 1999a, Johnson 1992, Turner *et al.* 1994), which use a statistical distribution of fire frequency to simulate fire occurrence. The hierarchical fire frequency model divides a fire occurrence into two consecutive events—fire ignition and fire initiation (fig. 4). A fire occurrence begins with an ignition attempt from an external heat source that heats the forest fuel complex up to its ignition temperature. Fire ignition agents are either natural (lightning) or anthropogenic (e.g., arson or accidental). A fire initiation event starts with the ignition and is successful when an area equal to the cell size is burned (Li 2000, 2001). Whether a fire ignition can result in fire initiation is dependent on the fuel loading, fuel arrangement, and fuel moisture content.

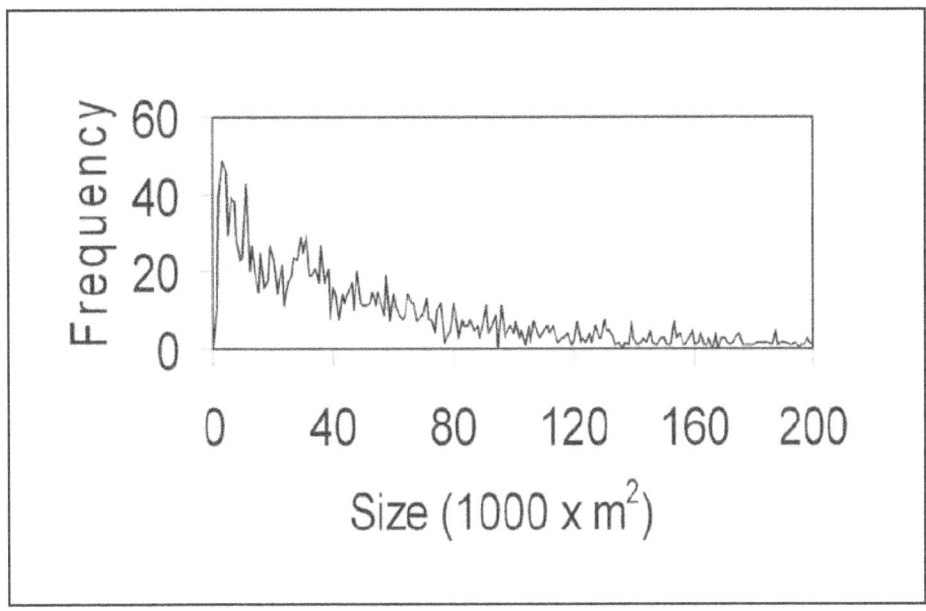

Figure 4. Fire size follows log-normal distribution with small fires occurring more frequently than large fires.

For a given time step (e.g., year 10), LANDIS first generates the number of ignitions (X) in the given fire regime unit from the Poisson distribution with the parameter ignition density λ (i.e., average fire ignitions per decade per hectare). For each ignition, LANDIS performs a Bernoulli trial, whose result is denoted by Y_i (ignition result), with the parameter fire initiation probability P_i, whose value is determined by the time since last fire of the ignited cell if the fuel module is turned off (equation 1), or fine fuel class if the fuel module is turned on (specified in fire parameter file):

$$P(t) = 1 - e^{-t/FC} \qquad (2)$$

where FC is fire cycle, t is time since last fire, and P is fire initiation probability. If the ignition becomes an initiation, we assign 1 to Y_i, otherwise we assign 0 to Y_i. The summation of the result of all ignitions generated for a given fire regime unit per decade ($\sum Y_i, i = 1,2,...,X$) is then the number of fire occurrences per decade for the given fire regime unit. For each initiation, LANDIS will randomly select a fire size, denoted by Z, from a log-normal distribution (fig. 4) with parameters μ (Mean Fire Size: MFS) and σ^2 (Standard Deviation of Fire Size: STD) to simulate fire spread. The overall structure is depicted in figure 5.

Since a landscape often consists of more than one fire regime unit, it is possible that a fire starts from one fire regime unit and spreads to another. When a fire reaches another fire regime unit, LANDIS will use a new fire ignition from the ignition pool of this new fire regime unit. If such a new ignition becomes a fire initiation, LANDIS will randomly draw another fire size from the fire size distribution defined on this new fire regime unit. Such a fire will be recorded as one single fire event in the fire log files, but it actually consists of two fire occurrences.

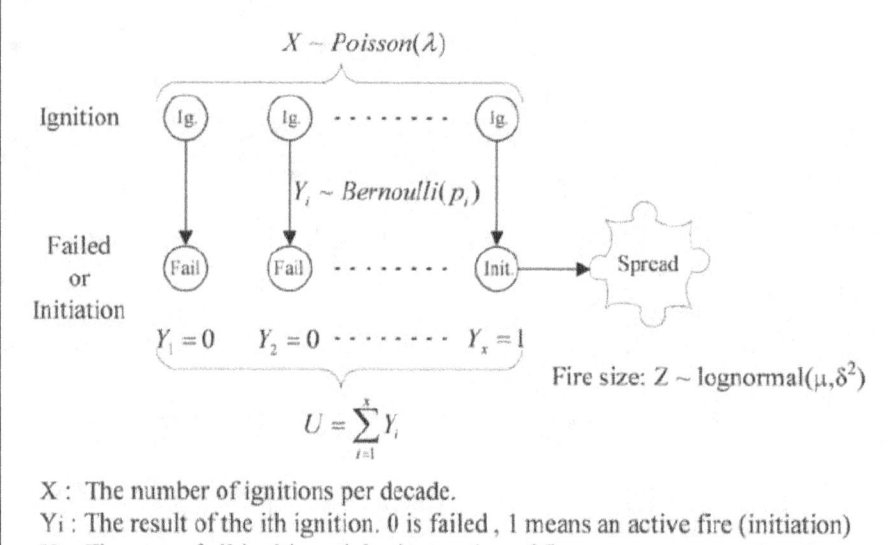

X : The number of ignitions per decade.

Y_i : The result of the ith ignition. 0 is failed , 1 means an active fire (initiation)

U : The sum of all ignition trials, the number of fire occurrences per decade

Z : Fire size

Figure 5. The overview of the fire occurrence simulation design.

9.5.3.2 Fire spread simulation

LANDIS 4.0 has two algorithms to simulate fire spread. The first one is a percolation algorithm similar to the algorithms of Gardner *et al.* (1999), Clarke *et al.* (1994), and Wimberley *et al.* (2000) to simulate fire spread. Fires simulated by the percolation algorithms spread from a burning cell to forested cells in the cardinal directions (up, down, left, and right). These cells are entered into a priority queue in a random order. The first cell in the queue has a higher priority of fire spread. The fire will continue to spread until it reaches its predetermined size. LANDIS does not allow a forested site to be burned more than once within one time step, and nonactive land types or ecoregions (e.g., roads, lakes) may serve as fuel breaks in the landscape. Therefore, it is possible for a fire to be extinguished prior to burning its predetermined size if the fire reaches fuel breaks or newly burned sites. In a real landscape, fires may spread across the boundaries of fire regime units where the fire size distribution changes. When a fire spreads into a different fire regime unit, the module will simulate a new ignition. If the new ignition results in an active fire, a new predetermined fire size will be selected based on the fire size distribution for the new fire regime unit.

The second algorithm used in LANDIS 4.0 is similar to Hargrove *et al.* (2000), a modified percolation method with a fire front, which can simulate fire spread behavior with respect to fuel configuration, topography, and prevailing wind. A fire front is defined as the part of a fire within which continuous flaming combustion is taking place. The fire front in LANDIS is assumed to be the edges of the fire perimeter. Fire will spread out from the fire front along eight directional (N, NE, E, SE, S, SW, W, NW) neighbor sites. The directional spread probability in each site is computed by its own fuel quality and quantity, biased with topographical aspect and slope, and wind direction and speed:

$$P = 1 - e^{-(1+r_1)^y (1+r_2)^z (1+r_3)^w kx} \qquad (3)$$

where r_1 is wind coefficient, which serves as an adjustment so that the user can increase or decrease wind effect on the directional spread probability calculation. If $r_1 = 0$, then there is no wind effect on the directional spread probability calculation no matter how much wind speed (y) is. Similarly, r_2 is the topography coefficient, r_3 is the predefined fire size distribution coefficient, and k is the fuel coefficient. In LANDIS parameter files, k is defined as the base probability for fuel class 3 (denoted by *prbase*) when there are no other factors on spread probability (i.e., r_1, r_2, r_3 are all 0). Equation 4 shows the relation between k and base probability:

$$k = \log(1 - prbase) / (-3) \qquad (4)$$

Equation 4 denotes the relation between fuel coefficient and base probability for fuel class 3. There are four independent variables in the fire spread probability π equation: y is wind speed class (0, 1, 2, 3, 4, 5), z is topographical slope ($-\pi/2$ to $\pi/2$), and x is fuel class (i.e., the potential fire intensity class (0, 1 ~ 5) in the fuel module). w is the predefined fire size effect, a normalized ratio of current fire size to predefined fire size (equation 5) used to determine how the current fire size affects fire spread probability. The range of w is 1 to negative infinity. However, in LANDIS practical simulations, w usually ranges from 1 (when current fire size equals 0) to –1 (when current size equals predefined size). It decreases as the current size increases, and reaches zero when fire spread reaches half of predefined size.

$$w = 1 - 2CS / FS \qquad (5)$$

where CS is current simulated fire size, and FS is predefined fire size.

9.5.3.3 Fire effect simulation

Fire intensity is determined by the quantity and quality of fuel. When the fuel module is turned off, a simple framework reflects the relationship between fuel quantity and years of accumulation on different fire regime units (i.e., fire curves defined for each fire regime unit level; refer to section 13.2 for details). Fire intensity is categorized into 6 classes (0 ~ 5, with a class 5 fire the most intense). When the fuel module is on, LANDIS will directly use potential fire-intensity class calculated in the fuel module instead.

Fire is a bottom-up disturbance, such that fires of low intensity affect only younger age classes. Also, fire tolerance varies among species fire-tolerance classes. To implement these two characteristics, species fire-tolerance classes, containing five categories from 1 to 5, are designed to reflect the differences of fire tolerance among species. Species fire-susceptibility classes are designed to reflect differences related to age. A fire of a given intensity interacts with individual species and age cohorts through the species fire tolerance and age susceptibility. The interactions of fire with species fire tolerance and age susceptibility have been explicitly defined in He and Mladenoff (1999a) (fig. 6).

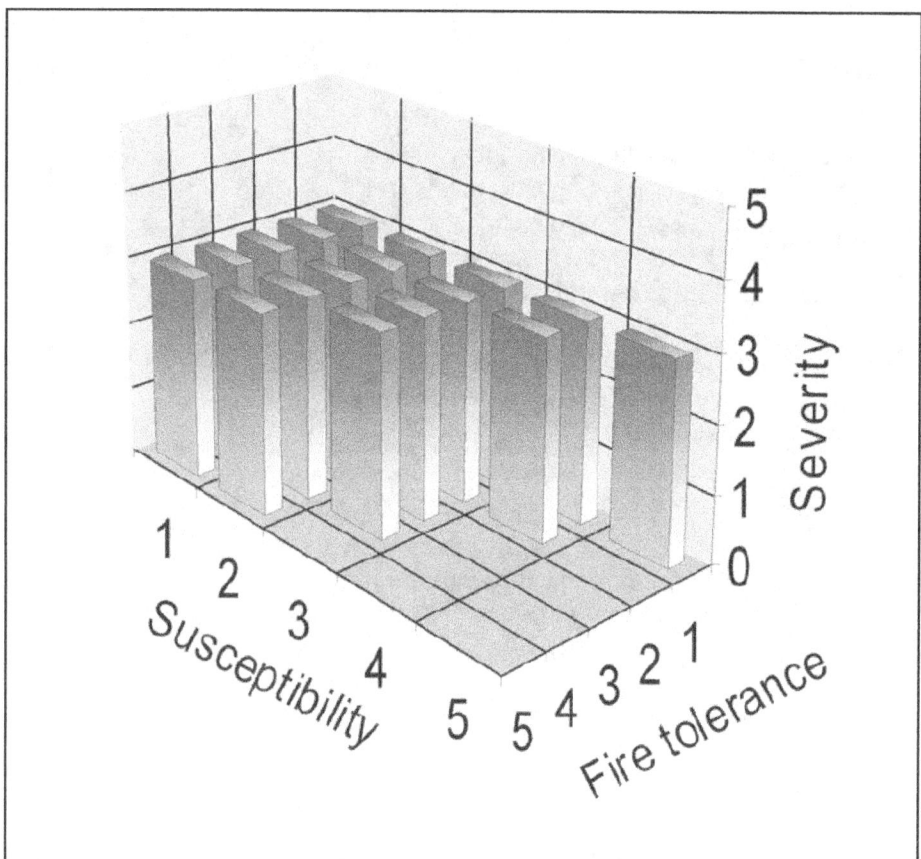

Figure 6. Fire intensity vs. fire tolerance (species classes) and susceptibility (age classes). Each individual bar represents the removal range of species of a given age class under fire-intensity class three.

9.5.4 Wind Disturbance

Wind disturbance follows an approach similar to fire, except that wind is a top-down disturbance, where species susceptibility increases with age and size (Mladenoff and He 1999). A wind disturbance event can add fine fuel and coarse fuel and influence the potential fire-intensity class, depending on the decomposition dynamics of the particular ecoregion. Interactions between these two disturbances can be interesting and complex. Generally, wind disturbance becomes more important on ecoregions with long-lived species, and where fire frequency is low.

Wind disturbance events are stochastic for a single site, but have repeated patterns in terms of breakout location, size, and shape at landscape scales. It has long been noted that some areas are more prone to wind disturbance than others. The differences are often represented by using mean wind-return intervals, i.e., the mean number of years for wind to recur on a given area. Similar to the approaches used in other studies, in LANDIS the mean wind-return interval is used to calculate wind probability using the following equation:

$$P = B \cdot lw \cdot MI^{-(e+2)} \qquad (6)$$

where P is the wind probability of a cell, MI is the mean wind return interval of a given ecoregion on which the cell resides, B is the wind probability coefficient designed for model calibration ($B=MI$ by default), and lw is the number of years since last wind on that cell. With the above distribution, P varies among ecoregions with MIs, and it can be further altered by lw recorded for each single cell. For example, if wind occurs at a given cell in a given time step, lw of the cell is reset to 0, and P for that cell is calculated as 0 during that time step. This eliminates the possibility of cells being blown down twice in the same time step regardless of how short MI is.

Another important feature of wind disturbance is wind size, defined from the following equation integrating random factors and the mean wind size:

$$S = A \cdot (10.0)^r \cdot MS \qquad (7)$$

where S is the wind size, MS is the mean wind size, A is the wind disturbance size coefficient designed for model calibration ($A=0.34$ by default), and r is a normalized random number. Under similar mean wind return interval, one can have very different wind regimes ranging from small, frequent wind to large, infrequent wind, which are defined by the distribution of S.

9.5.5 Harvest

The timber harvest capability of LANDIS allows flexible simulation of the broad spectrum of silvicultural activities that are commonly implemented on managed forests (Gustafson *et al.* 2000). These capabilities are simulated across two distinct hierarchies of disturbance intensity and the spatial configuration. The intensity of management activity ranges from thinning through single-tree selective harvest to clearcutting. The specific details of how these activities affect species and cohort structure are controlled by the user, allowing an almost infinite range of management activity to be simulated. The spatial configuration of management activity is controlled by the designation of Management Areas (MA) in which distinct management activities and intensities can be simulated on the stands within that MA (fig. 7).

LANDIS implements timber harvest within a specific hierarchical management structure. The overall landscape is divided into MAs, each to be treated with specific harvest regimes at specific intensities. The MAs need not be contiguous (i.e., multiple areas having the same MA designation may be delineated). Furthermore, some management units may be specified to have no harvest at all. Harvesting on land in other ownerships can be simulated by representing those ownerships as distinct MAs.

Within MAs that are to be harvested, LANDIS expects to find the land base delineated into stands. These are represented by a map layer in which stand polygons have been gridded so that each site (where site is the equivalent of a cell or a pixel in the raster) has the value of the stand ID number. Often, land in other ownerships will be interspersed among these stands. Any lands that will never have harvests allocated on them can be represented by zeros in the stand map. Based on the map layers of MAs and stands, each site becomes associated with an MA and a stand ID.

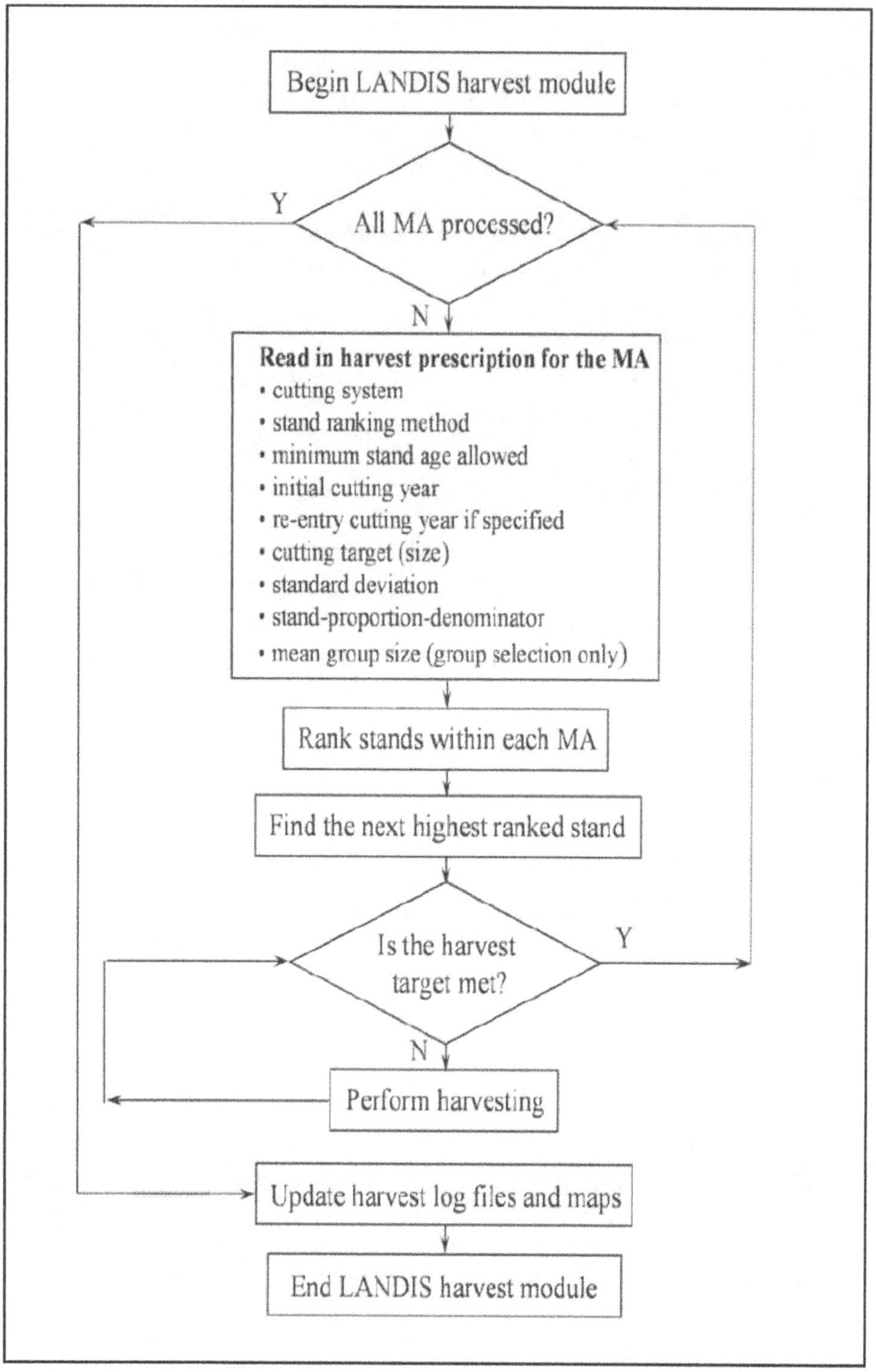

```
              ┌─────────────────────────────────┐
              │   Begin LANDIS harvest module   │
              └─────────────────────────────────┘
                              │
                              ▼
          Y  ◄──────────⟨   All MA processed?   ⟩◄──────────
                              │ N
                              ▼
       ┌───────────────────────────────────────────┐
       │   Read in harvest prescription for the MA  │
       │   • cutting system                         │
       │   • stand ranking method                   │
       │   • minimum stand age allowed              │
       │   • initial cutting year                   │
       │   • re-entry cutting year if specified     │
       │   • cutting target (size)                  │
       │   • standard deviation                     │
       │   • stand-proportion-denominator           │
       │   • mean group size (group selection only) │
       └───────────────────────────────────────────┘
                              │
                              ▼
              ┌─────────────────────────────────┐
              │   Rank stands within each MA    │
              └─────────────────────────────────┘
                              │
                              ▼
              ┌─────────────────────────────────┐
              │ Find the next highest ranked stand│
              └─────────────────────────────────┘
                              │
                              ▼
                  ⟨   Is the harvest   ⟩  Y ──────►
                  ⟨    target met?     ⟩
                              │ N
                              ▼
              ┌─────────────────────────────────┐
              │       Perform harvesting        │
              └─────────────────────────────────┘
                              │
                              ▼
              ┌─────────────────────────────────┐
              │  Update harvest log files and maps│
              └─────────────────────────────────┘
                              │
                              ▼
              ┌─────────────────────────────────┐
              │    End LANDIS harvest module    │
              └─────────────────────────────────┘
```

Figure 7. Flow chart of the LANDIS harvest module show harvest actions with one LANDIS iteration.

Harvests are implemented by removing specific cohorts of specific species on sites selected for harvest. The sites selected for harvest are determined by one of eight "harvest regimes" from which the user may choose. These harvest regimes vary in the number of entries required to complete the silvicultural treatment, and in whether they are applied to: 1) an entire stand (stand-filling), 2) a portion of a stand or to multiple stands (stand-spreading), and 3) multiple patches within a

single stand (i.e., group selection). The regimes currently available are:
1) one-entry, stand-filling, 2) periodic-entry, stand-resampling, stand-filling,
3) two-entry, stand-filling, 4) one-entry, stand-spreading, 5) two-entry, stand-spreading, 6) periodic-entry, group selection, 7) periodic-entry-fixed stand, two-entry, stand-filling, and 8) periodic-entry-stand-resampling, two-entry, stand-filling. Stand resampling means that in each entry year, the stands within the management area will be ranked again using the initial ranking algorithm. Thus, the specific stands treated in each entry may vary, but the treatment applied will not.

These regimes allow simulation of multiple-entry silvicultural treatments such as shelterwood, seed-tree, and group selection. The periodic entry options allow for automatic harvesting of stands at some specified interval (e.g., rotation length). Stand-filling regimes are applied to every site in a single stand, while stand-spreading regimes begin at a focal site in a stand; harvest terminates when a certain harvest size is reached. This size may be reached before the stand is completely harvested, or the harvest may spill over into an adjacent stand. All eligible sites within a stand must be harvested before harvest can spill over into another stand, but the process may continue until the size has been reached. This feature allows timber management to be used to change the patch size distribution of the landscape, and to allow patterns to emerge that are less constrained by the underlying stand map than are the stand-filling harvest regimes.

Stands for the application of these regimes are selected using a ranking algorithm chosen by the user. Stands within each MA are prioritized for harvest (ranked) according to rules that reflect criteria that might be used by forest planners or researchers. The ranking algorithms currently include Stand Age (oldest first), Economic Importance (most valuable stands first), Regulate Age Class Distribution (attempt to produce an even distribution), and Random (choose stands randomly). Because stands are ranked independently for each MA, different ranking algorithms can be applied to different MAs. When an adjacent stand needs to be harvested by a stand-spreading regime, the highest ranked of all the adjacent stands is selected.

Variation in the intensity of harvest activity is controlled by rules governing the removal of age cohorts of species found on the site being harvested. The rules for each harvest regime are specified by the user in the form of removal masks that for each species specify which age cohorts (if present on the site) are to be removed. For example, the prescribed burning mask might specify that the youngest cohort of all species be removed. A shelterwood mask might specify that all cohorts be removed for all species except one or two older cohorts of one or two species during the first entry, and all older cohorts during the second entry. Because the removal masks are generated by the user, the user has unlimited flexibility to tailor the masks to the treatments to be simulated and the characteristics of the species found on the landscape.

The extent of harvesting is controlled by the user. For each MA the user must specify the regimes to be applied, the total area to be harvested under each regime, and the ranking algorithm to be used for each regime. If a stand-spreading regime is chosen, the user must specify the size distribution for the harvests. Simulations are controlled by a parameter input file. Once this file is produced, it can be modified to introduce changes to the scenario simulated, allowing alternatives and replicates to be readily generated.

The Harvest module completes two major loops to simulate one time period of timber harvest: 1) It sequentially visits each MA in which timber harvest is prescribed, and 2) within each MA, it sequentially simulates each harvest regime specified for that MA, beginning with scheduled re-entries. Different harvesting rules can be specified for each MA. For each harvest regime, the module allocates harvests to stands until the target number of sites has been allocated. The order in which stands are chosen is determined by the ranking procedure. At the completion of the model run, LANDIS produces a log file allowing comparison of the harvest targets with the allocations actually made. LANDIS also creates output files that report how many sites containing each cohort (by species) were cut (useful to estimate volume and value generated by harvest activity), and how many sites containing cohorts (by species) remain on each stand (useful to estimate stand vertical structure).

9.5.6 Biological Disturbance Agent (BDA)

Biological disturbances, such as insect and disease outbreaks, are critically important agents of forest change that cause tree mortality at scales ranging from individual trees of a single species to entire regions. The BDA module is designed to simulate tree mortality following major outbreaks of insects and/or disease, where major outbreaks are defined as those significant enough to influence forest succession, fire disturbance, or harvest disturbance at landscape scales.

Biological disturbances in LANDIS are probabilistic at the site (i.e., cell) scale, where each site is assigned a probability value called *biological disturbance probability (BDP)* and compared with a uniform random number to determine whether the site is disturbed or not. Disturbance causes species- and cohort-specific mortality in the cell. In the simplest case, BDP equals *Site Resource Dominance*, a number that ranges from 0 (no host) to 1 (most preferred host) based on the tree species and age cohorts present on the site. Four additional optional factors may also modify BDP: 1) environmental and/or other disturbance-related stress (*Site Resource Modifiers*); 2) the abundance of host in the neighborhood surrounding the site (*Neighborhood Resource Dominance*); 3) user-defined temporal functions (e.g., cyclic, random, or chronic) that affect the temporal pattern of disturbances across the entire spatial domain of the simulation (*Regional Outbreak Status*); and 4) spatial epidemic zones defined via simulated dispersal of a BDA through a heterogeneous landscape (*Dispersal*). The above combinations of optional factors allow the BDA module to accommodate several types of destructive insect and disease species, and more than one BDA may be simulated concurrently to examine their interactions.

More detail on the BDA module and its behavior can be found in Sturtevant *et al.* (2004). However, several key terms were modified from this publication to be consistent with the terminology of other natural disturbance modules in LANDIS 4.0. In this users guide, we use the term BDP for site vulnerability, and all references to "vulnerability" or "susceptibility" in Sturtevant *et al.* (2004) have been changed here to either tolerance class (for species) or susceptibility class (for species age cohort). The rank order of these two classes is also consistent with the design of the other natural disturbance modules. Finally, all references in Sturtevant *et al.* (2004) to the "severity" class of a disturbance have been changed here to "intensity" class.

9.5.6.1 Site resource dominance

Site resource dominance (SRD) indicates the relative quantity/quality of food resources on a given site and is a combined function of tree species composition and the age cohorts present on that site. The relative resource value of a given species cohort is defined by its host preference class, where preferred host = 1.0, secondary host = 0.66, minor host = 0.33, and nonhost = 0. The BDA module compares a look-up table (see section 14.2) with the species cohort list generated by LANDIS to calculate SRD using one of two methods: 1) SRD = the maximum host preference class present, or 2) SRD = the average resource value of all tree species present, where the resource value of each species is represented by the cohort with the oldest host preference.

9.5.6.2 Site resource modifiers

Site resource modifiers are optional parameters used to adjust SRD to reflect variation in the quality of food resources introduced by site environment (i.e., land type) and recent disturbance. Both land type modifiers (LTMs) and disturbance modifiers (DMs) can range between –1 and +1, and will be added to the SRD value of all active sites where host species are present. LTMs are assumed to be constant for the entire simulation, while DMs decline linearly with the time since last disturbance. Disturbances that may affect a given BDA include fire and wind. Disturbance effects from another BDA and user-specified harvest prescriptions are currently not implemented. SRD is then modified by LTM and the sum of all DMs:

$$SRD_m = SRD + LTM + (DM_{wind} + DM_{fire} + ...) \qquad (8)$$

The user should calibrate the above modifiers to reflect the relative influence of species composition/age structure, the abiotic environment, and recent disturbance. For example, an LTM value of 0.33 is equal to a full step increase in disturbance intensity above that calculated using species composition alone (see section 14).

9.5.6.3 Neighborhood resource dominance

Several recent studies suggest that the landscape context of a site also influences the probability and intensity of disturbance (Cappuccino *et al.* 1998, Radeloff *et al.* 2000). A neighborhood effect is modeled in LANDIS as the mean SRD_m of each cell within a user-defined radius R, using one of three radial distance weighting functions listed in increasing order of local dominance: uniform, linear, and Gaussian (Orr 1996; see Sturtevant *et al.* 2004). Neighborhood resource dominance (NRD) is calculated for all sites containing host species (i.e., SRD > 0). An optional subsampling procedure calculates the NRD for every other site, and the NRD of the remaining sites are estimated by the mean NRD of adjacent sites in the four cardinal directions. For large neighborhoods, this subsampling routine can increase the processing speed of the BDA by over 40 percent (Sturtevant *et al.* 2004).

9.5.6.4 Regional outbreak status

Several simple temporal patterns may be simulated in the BDA module to represent general outbreak trends for the entire study landscape. Temporal patterns in a given BDA are assumed constant for the length of the simulation, and are defined by a suite of temporal disturbance functions that define the landscape scale intensity of the BDA at a given time step, termed Regional Outbreak Status (ROS). ROS units are integer classes ranging from 0 (no outbreak) to 3 (intense outbreak). The time to the next outbreak is calculated following each outbreak event using either a uniform or a normal random function. Though the actual time periods between outbreaks will be constrained by the time step of LANDIS (currently set at 10 years), the random outbreak functions may be used to vary the outbreak interval so that the *average* interval between outbreaks observed during the length of the simulation approximates that expected by the user.

The magnitude of simulated regional outbreaks is controlled by the MinROS and MaxROS parameters. MinROS defines the "background" outbreak activity that will occur in each time step. Outbreak type ("TempType" in the BDA parameter file) determines whether outbreaks are binary (either MinROS or MaxROS; TempType = "pulse") or if the ROS can range between those values (TempType = "variable pulse"). For the variable pulse outbreak type, the ROS value is randomly selected for each outbreak event from the range between MinROS+1 and MaxROS.

9.5.6.5 BDA effects

Both the probability that a site is disturbed by a given BDA and the intensity of that disturbance are controlled by biological disturbance probability (BDP). BDP is defined by the following equation:

$$BDP = a \cdot \{[SRD_m + (NRD*NW)]/(1+NW)\} \cdot (ROS/3) \qquad (9)$$

where a is a user-defined calibration parameter (by default, a should = 1); SRD_m = the species and age composition of the site (SRD), optionally modified by land type and/or past disturbance (equation 8); NRD = the mean SRD_m of sites within the neighborhood surrounding a site; NW = Neighborhood Weight, a parameter designed to define the relative importance between site and neighborhood resources; and ROS = Regional Outbreak Status.

Sites are selected for disturbance by comparing BDP with a uniform random number ranging from 0-1. Note that while equation 8 (see section 9.5.5.2) allows SRD_m to exceed 1.0, by definition BDP cannot exceed 1.0 (i.e., 100 percent probability of disturbance). SRD_m values exceeding 1.0 can therefore only further enhance the probability of disturbance if additional variables such as neighborhoods or temporal disturbance functions are applied. Once a site is disturbed, the disturbance intensity class is calculated for the site to determine which species cohorts die, based on their tolerance class. Disturbance intensity is a direct function of BDP, where BDP < 0.33 = intensity class 1; 0.33 < BDP < 0.67 = intensity class 2; BDP > 0.67 = intensity class 3 disturbance. Unlike fire or wind disturbance, there is no predefined function that estimates susceptibility class as a function of species tolerance class. Instead, susceptibility class is defined directly by a look-up table similar to that used for host preference class (see section 9.5.6.1). Cohort mortality follows these rules: intensity class 1 disturbance kills all susceptibility class 1 cohorts, intensity class 2 disturbance kills susceptibility classes 1 and 2, and intensity class 3 disturbance kills susceptibility classes 1-3. Susceptibility class 4 species age cohorts, including all nonhost species, cannot be disturbed by the BDA. If no other BDA options are simulated, the BDA module finishes by updating species cohort lists, updating the time since last biological disturbance, outputting a map of BDA disturbance events, and updating the BDA log (fig. 8).

9.5.6.6 BDA dispersal

Some epidemics occur at spatial scales smaller than the typical simulation area of LANDIS. Accounting for BDA dispersal and spread will be necessary for these cases. The BDA dispersal procedure defines smaller spatial zones within the modeled landscape where BDA disturbance may occur within a given time step. Within these restricted spatial zones, the BDA operates exactly the same as if the outbreak were synchronous. Note that the dispersal procedures for the BDA module are still under development, but there are some preliminary dispersal procedures available in LANDIS 4.0.

9.5.6.6.1 Epicenters

Epicenters are defined as central sites from which a BDA may disperse. There are three types of epicenters: 1) initial epicenters—sites randomly selected at time = 0 to initiate new outbreak zones in the first time step; 2) seed epicenters—sites randomly selected at each time step an outbreak occurs to initiate new outbreak zones outside the outbreak zone defined at time $t–1$ during the simulation; and 3) outbreak zone epicenters—sites randomly selected from within the last outbreak zone (i.e., time = $t–1$) to continue the spread of an outbreak in consecutive time steps. The BDA module will randomly select epicenters from a subset of sites that are above user-specified threshold site

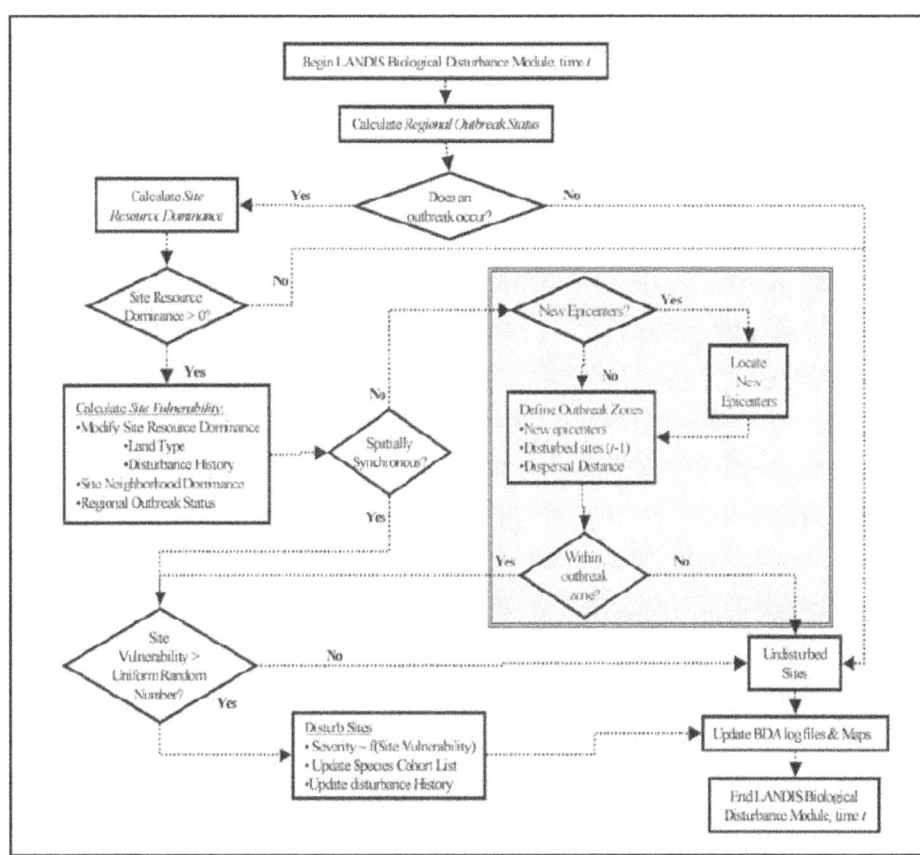

Figure 8. BDA flow diagram.

vulnerability. Initial epicenters can be selected anywhere in the landscape where sites meet this criterion; seed and outbreak zone epicenters are selected from outside and inside (respectively) the outbreak zone defined at time $t–1$.

The number of initial epicenters is a simple user-defined parameter. The following negative exponential equation determines how many new epicenters will be generated both inside and outside existing outbreak zones:

$$Y_i = A_i * \exp(-c_i X_i) \qquad (10)$$

Here, A_i = the number of qualified potential epicenter sites (i.e., the number of sites either inside or outside the last outbreak zone where BDP > the epidemic threshold), X_i = the current number of selected epicenters of a given type, and Y_i = the number of remaining sites that can be checked. Coefficient c_i is a user-defined parameter that controls statistically how many new epicenters may be generated for either seed epicenter or outbreak zone epicenter type. The number of epicenters will decrease with increasing c.

9.5.6.6.2 Spatial outbreak zones

Outbreak zones are defined using dispersal routines that spread from an epicenter to a circular boundary with a radius defined by the annual dispersal distance of a BDA, multiplied by the number of years in a time step (i.e., 10). An outbreak zone either automatically expands to this maximum limit (termed "regular dispersal") or occurs as a percolation process through a binary landscape, where it may only spread through sites containing host tree species. Ability to spread over nonhost cells is defined by a user-defined neighborhood rule (*sensu* Gardner 1999) termed a "structuring element" in the BDA Module. Available structuring elements include 4, 8, 12, and 24 nearest neighbors (fig. 9).

The dispersal routines will attempt to spread each epicenter to its maximum dispersal distance using the neighborhood rule defined by the user. An outbreak zone from a given epicenter may overlap one created from a nearby epicenter. The cumulative area of all zones created during the time step defines the spatial extent over which the BDA may disturb sites during that time step.

9.5.7 Fuel and fuel management

The LANDIS fuel module is a new addition to LANDIS. It tracks fine fuel, coarse fuel, and live fuels, simulates various fuel management practices, and estimates the impact of fuel reduction activities (He *et al.* 2004). In the fuel module, fine fuels (FF) represent primarily foliage litter fall and small dead twigs

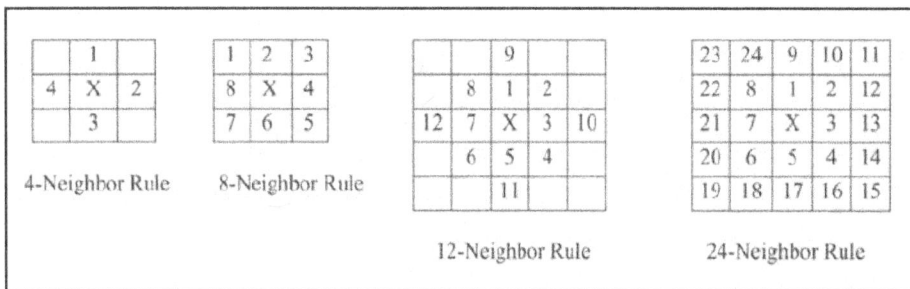

Figure 9. Available structuring elements.

less than ¼ inch in diameter. They are the primary prerequisite for fire ignitions. Coarse fuels (CF) include any dead tree materials that have a diameter ≥ 3 inches. These include snags, stems, boles, harvest stumps, and standing dead trees, which affect the intensity class of fire. Live fuels, also called canopy fuels, are live trees that may be ignited during high intensity fires (e.g., crown fires).

9.5.7.1 Fine fuel

Calculating the amount of fine fuel involves deriving a fine fuel amount based on species age and modified by the fuel quality coefficient (FQC). Fine fuel from different species may have different flammability due to differences in physical and chemical attributes (Brown *et al.* 1982). We use a fuel quality coefficient ($0 < FQC <= 1$) to summarize such differences on a relative scale. Species with low FQC contribute less to the flammability of fine fuels than species with high FQC. FQCs are ranked and parameterized by users, and the same value (e.g., $FQC=1$) can be used for all species if there are no discernible differences among species. The result is not the absolute quantity of fine fuels, but rather an "effective index" of the amount of fine fuel that accounts for its flammability. If there are n species in a cell, the total amount of fine fuel (FF) in this cell is calculated as

$$FF = (\sum_{i=1}^{n} Age_i / Long_i \cdot FQC_i) / n \qquad (11)$$

where Age_i is the age of the oldest cohort of the ith species, $Long_i$ is the maximum longevity of the ith species (also used elsewhere in LANDIS), and FQC is as previously defined. Dividing by n averages the amount of fuel across all species present in the cell. Because LANDIS tracks only the presence and absence of species/age cohorts, the design for simulating fine fuels assumes that all species present in a cell have the same density. Such an assumption may not be realistic for individual cells, but at the landscape scale with millions of cells, relative species abundance can be realistically approximated (He *et al.* 1998). Fine fuel production changes through the lifespan of a given species. In this example (fig. 10), the amount of fine fuel created by each species (the thin line) is positively correlated with age until approximately 70 percent of the species lifespan is reached, and becomes negatively correlated with age as the species age approaches maximum species longevity. The actual value calculated is translated into five categorical fine fuel classes using the user-defined relationship (fig. 10, see section 15.3). Such relationships can be defined for each species and specific ecosystems based upon empirical data.

9.5.7.2 Coarse fuels

Unlike fine fuels, coarse fuels are not derived using species-specific age cohorts. Instead, stand age (the oldest age cohorts) in combination with disturbance history (time since last disturbance) is used to determine the coarse fuel accumulation for a cell (Brown and See 1981, Harmon *et al.* 1986, Spetich *et al.* 1999, Spies *et al.* 1988, Sturtevant *et al.* 1997). Coarse fuel amount is the interplay between input and decomposition (Spies *et al.* 1988, Sturtevant *et al.* 1997). Such interplay may vary by land type (Harmon *et al.* 1986), which encapsulate environmental variables (e.g., climate, soil, slope, and aspect) (fig. 10).

In the absence of disturbance, the accumulation process dominates until the amount of coarse fuel reaches a level where decomposition and accumulation

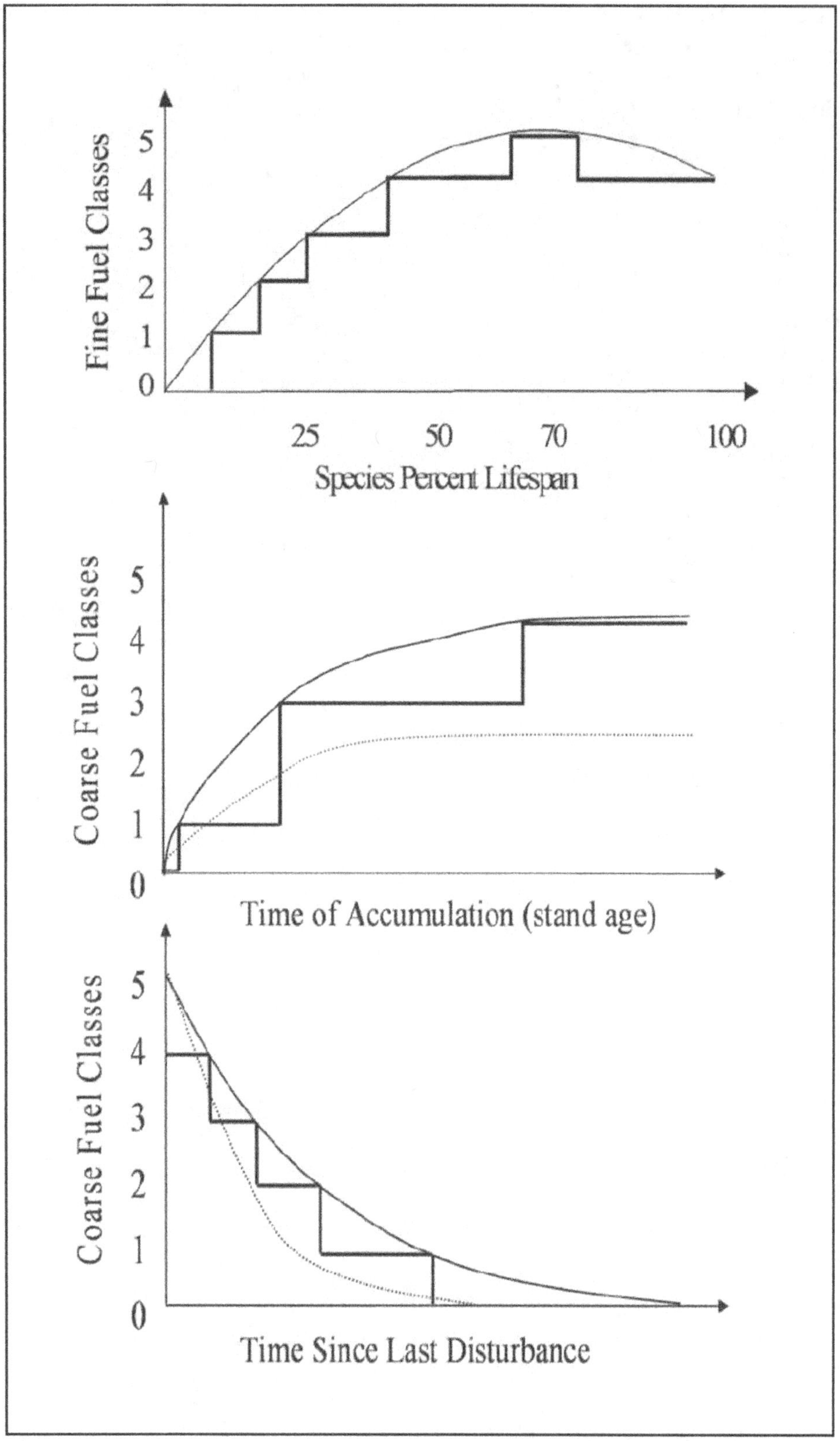

Figure 10. Fine fuel and coarse fuel accumulation and decomposition. The relationship can be further modified by land type, disturbance, harvest, and fuel treatment.

are in balance (Bergeron and Flannigan 2000, Sturtevant *et al.* 1997), as depicted in figure 10. For example, on a mesic land type with high decomposition rates, the amount of coarse fuel can be low, whereas on a xeric land type with low decomposition rates, the amount of coarse fuel can be high. The decomposition process is modeled using the decomposition curve as described in previous studies (Foster and Lang 1982, Hale and Pastor 1998, Lambert *et al.* 1980, MacMillan 1988) (fig. 10). Such a decomposition curve is also user-defined for each land type. The example suggests two decomposition trajectories of coarse fuels on two different land types (fig. 10).

The accumulation and decomposition curves together form the general "U-shaped" temporal pattern observed in many forest ecosystems (Spetich *et al.* 1999, Sturtevant *et al.* 1997). In many boreal and northern hardwood forest ecosystems, a land type can seldom accumulate enough coarse fuel to reach class five unless there are other disturbance events occurring such as wind, BDA, and/or harvest. Users can define these disturbance-related accumulations using coarse fuel accumulation and decomposition curves (fig. 10).

Due to the long temporal scales involved in estimating the amount of coarse fuels, uncertainty is high. Collapsing the estimates of the quantity of coarse fuel into five categorical classes (very low to very high) reduces the potential for false precision and the parameterization burden for the module.

The elapsed time of fuel accumulation (TFC) is used to determine the current amount of coarse fuel as shown in figure 10. The various modifiers, once activated, will determine how much the coarse fuel class is increased or reduced. The relationships defined for each modifier (section 15.2) and the decomposition status defined in figure 10 is used to determine the final coarse fuel amount. The highest class (up to class 5) will be retained as the final coarse fuel class. For example, based upon the time of coarse fuel accumulation for a site, the coarse fuel class is determined to be class 2. However, an intense wind disturbance and an insect defoliation would each raise the coarse fuel class by 3 (e.g., section 15.2). This leads to a final coarse fuel class for this site that is larger than 5 (2+3+3). In such a case, the model will set the coarse fuel class to 5.

9.5.7.3 Fine fuel and coarse fuel modifier

Land type, fire, wind, harvest, and biological disturbance can modify the fine fuel and coarse fuel classes derived from the relationships discussed above. Fine fuel decomposition rates may vary by land types (Agee and Huff 1987). Thus, a land type modifier may decrease or increase the fine fuel class derived from species age cohorts. For example, a fine fuel class 3 on a mesic land type might decrease to class 2 because the decomposition rate is relatively high, while the same fuel class (3) on a xeric land type might increase to class 4, since the decomposition rate is relatively low. The user defines the modifier in the fuel module input file, and the default is no modification. Disturbances may increase or decrease the fuel class in a similar way. For example, as a parameter for a Biological Disturbance Agent (BDA) (e.g., insect pest), the user defines how a BDA disturbance event will increase the fine fuel and coarse fuel class, depending on the type and intensity of the event. Similarly, fire events can reduce the fine and coarse fuel class (Armour *et al.* 1984) based on user-defined rules. The simplest and most common case is that fires remove all fine fuels. Alternatively, a rule could remove fine and coarse fuels in proportion to the intensity class of the fire. Wind disturbances primarily increase coarse fuel. However, they can also increase fine fuels by producing dead leaves and needles. Increases in fine fuel classes caused by wind can be determined by the intensity class of the wind. Harvest activities can also modify the fine and coarse fuel class. The user can also define how each harvest prescription defined in the Harvest module will modify the fine and coarse fuel class.

9.5.7.4 Potential fire intensity

Potential fire intensity is determined by the combination of fine fuel and coarse fuel in each cell. A set of rules can be defined (see section 15.3.1) based upon the assumption that coarse fuel is the primary contributor to the fire intensity class, since in many forest ecosystems coarse fuel accounts for about 90 percent of forest floor mass (Grier and Logan 1977, Lambert *et al.* 1980, Lang and Forman 1978). Users can define other rules according to the ecosystems they study. In the example in section 15.3.1, high-intensity fires are not common compared to low-intensity fires. Seven fine and coarse fuel combinations result in fire intensity = 1 (very low), seven in fire intensity = 2, six in fire intensity = 3, three in fire intensity = 4, and two in fire intensity = 5 (very high) (see section 15.3.1).

9.5.7.5 Live fuel-fire intensity modifier

Live fuels are live trees that may be ignited in high-intensity fire situations (such as crown fires). Thus, live fuels can be a fire intensity modifier. A mid-level intensity fire (≥ 3) may change into a crown fire (intensity class = 5) if there are suitable conifer species present (e.g., FQC=1). However, changing from low-intensity fire to crown fire is not a deterministic event and a probability function is used to predict its occurrence. For example, the probability of low-intensity fire changing to a crown fire is 0.01-0.05 based on the empirical knowledge for Missouri central hardwoods (B. Cutter, Department of Forestry, University of Missouri-Columbia, personal communication). Such a probability (P) can be user defined. In the fuel module, when fire intensity reaches level 3 and there are species with $FQC = 1$ present, the fire intensity can reach 5 if the uniform random number $>P$.

9.5.7.6 Potential fire risk

Fire risk has a variety of definitions under different modeling frameworks. In the Fire Regime Condition Class, fire risk is defined as the risk of loss of key ecosystem components (Hardy *et al.* 2001). In the National Fire Plan, fire risk refers to the risk that communities and environment will experience a damaging fire (www.nwfireplan.gov). When the Forest Service forecasts fire risk, it defines that risk as the probability or chance of fire starting determined by weather index. In LANDIS 4.0, the definition of fire risk reflects the two key aspects: 1) the probability of fire occurrence, and 2) the intensity and spread once a fire ignition occurs (He *et al.* 2004). Fire probability is derived from the fire cycle and the time since last fire for each cell and is intended to account for climate and other factors that can influence ignition probability, whereas fire intensity and spread are related to biotic factors affecting the level of various fuels (Yang *et al.* 2004). In the LANDIS 4.0 fuel module, fire probability is converted into five classes, from very low to very high, based upon the "equal area" (the fire probability density function is divided into 5 areas of equal size) or equal interval approach. Potential fire intensity is determined by the combination of fine fuel and coarse fuel in each cell (see section 9.5.7.4).

Fire risk is classified into five classes based upon fire probability and fire intensity, from very low (class 1) to very high (class 5). We assume that potential fire probability and fire intensity equally contribute to the fire risk. Thus, in the default fire risk table (see section 15.3.3), five unique combinations of fire probability and potential intensity classes are identified for each fire risk class. Again, users can define this table based upon the characteristics of their study area. The module allows users to track the high fire risk areas on the landscape over time and to explore the effects of various fuel load reduction methods on the spatial and temporal dynamics of fire risk.

9.5.7.7 Fuel management

9.5.7.7.1 Treatment size, interval, and intensity

The LANDIS fuel module simulates fuel management practices that fall into two categories: prescribed burning and physical fuel load reduction (removal and mechanical thinning). LANDIS fuel management has spatial, temporal, and treatment components. The spatial component uses parameters on the desired treatment size (e.g., the percent area of a management unit to be treated) and determines where such a treatment can be spatially allocated (e.g., how stands are selected for treatments). The allocation criteria can be based upon rankings of potential fire risk, where stands with highest potential fire risk are treated first, or by using random selection. The temporal component of fuel management determines what year (decade) a given treatment is performed and how often it is repeated. Single, multiple, or periodical entry years can be specified. The treatment component specifies the treatment types (e.g., prescribed burning) and treatment intensity. Since the three components are independent, combinations of the three are capable of simulating most fuel treatment practices (He *et al.* 2004, Shang *et al.* 2004).

9.5.7.7.2 Prescribed burning

In LANDIS, prescribed burning mainly affects fine fuel, but it can also reduce coarse fuel based upon the user specification. The choice of low- vs. high-intensity prescribed burning treatments depends on the field conditions, resources, and potential fire risk (Brose and Wade 2002). For example, a low-intensity prescribed burning might reduce the fine fuel load by a maximum of 2 classes. A high-intensity prescribed burn might remove most fine fuel loads (reduced to 1).

9.5.7.7.3 Physical fuel load reduction

Mechanical thinning primarily targets coarse fuels, including reducing the fuel size and removing/reducing coarse fuel load. The low-intensity treatment reduces coarse fuel load by 1-2 classes when the coarse fuel class is >3. The high-intensity treatment removes most coarse fuels (reduced to class 1).

9.5.7.7.4 Other fuel treatments

The following example illustrates how to specify chipping and thinning of coarse fuel. The chipping and thinning treatment is prescribed only for high (=4) and very high (=5) coarse fuel classes, and classes 4 and 5 are reduced to class 2. Note that coarse fuel treatments can result in an increase in fine fuels. In this example, all fine fuel classes are increased by 1.

Coarse fuel load class before treatment:	0	1	2	3	4	5
Coarse fuel load class after treatment:	0	1	2	3	2	2
Fine fuel load class before treatment:	0	1	2	3	4	5
Fine fuel load class after treatment:	1	2	3	4	5	5

10.   OPERATING SYSTEMS AND CONFIGURATIONS

10.1 Operating Systems

LANDIS 4.0 is a 32-bit Windows application implemented with Visual C++. It runs under Windows 2000/XP with at least 215 MB of memory. There is no UNIX version of LANDIS 4.0.

10.2 Memory and Storage

The LANDIS 4.0 runs with 256 MB of internal memory. However, most runs will require substantially more RAM. If the necessary RAM is not available, virtual memory will be automatically allocated on the hard drive. Successful runs on large models have been performed on computers with 512 MB to 1 GB RAM. However, 1 GB or more RAM is recommended.

11.   BASIC LANDIS INPUT FILES

This section will describe basic LANDIS input files that are required to conduct a model run. Basic LANDIS input files are always needed regardless of which disturbance and management modules are turned on or off. LANDIS input files for individual disturbance and management processes will be discussed in subsequent chapters.

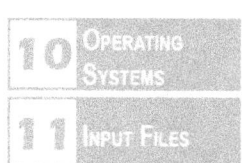

11.1 Parameter File (parameter.dat)

The parameter file is an entry file in ASCII format. It contains the settings of simulation scenarios such as number of years of simulation, dispersal mode, and particular processes simulated. Comments can be included in the parameter file as well as in any other attribute files. They can be located anywhere in a file as long as they are bracketed by the "#" character. The sequence of the parameters in the parameter file is fixed. The following is an example of a parameter input file, in which the first column stands for various parameters and the second column contains the brief explanations of each parameter.

```
species.dat        #1. Species life history attribute file#
landType.dat       #2. Attributes describing each land type class#
landType.gis       #3. 8- or 16-bit ERDAS GIS map of land type or ecoregion#
speciesMap.gis     #4. 8- or 16-bit ERDAS GIS map of species and age cohort classes#
mapAttribute.dat   #5. Attributes describing each map class#
mapIndex.dat       #6. Map names for tree species or forest cover output#
ageIndex.dat       #7. Age map name for output#
c:\project\output  #8. Path for LANDIS output#
default.plt        #9. Required in the parameter file directory#
frequency.dat      #10. Required in the parameter file directory#
50                 #11. Number of iterations (10 year time steps)#
1                  #12. 0 - generate randomly; other - fixed seed#
30                 #13. Cell size in meters#
DISPERSAL          #14. The name of the seed dispersal routine#
windInit.dat       #15. Flag-on of wind. N/A for flag-off#
fireInit.dat       #16. Flag-on of fire. N/A for flag-off#
BDAInit.dat        #17. Flag-on of BDA. N/A for flag-off#
fuelInit.dat       #18. Flag-on of fuel module. N/A for flag-off#
harvestInit.dat.   #19. Flag-on of wind disturbance. N/A for flag-off#
```

- The first 7 lines of the file are names of auxiliary LANDIS input files.

- Line 8 is the output directory name. All LANDIS output will be placed in this directory. If the last level of the directory does not exist, it will be created at run time. If more than one level of the path does not exist, LANDIS will generate an error message. Full descriptions of subsidiary files are in the following sections of documentation.

- Line 9 is a predefined LANDIS input file that defines the color palettes of various LANDIS output maps. These color palettes will be used only if the user explicitly informs the LANDIS Viewer or a GIS to do so.

- Line 10 is the LANDIS output frequency file that can be modified to affect the model output intervals for various processes.

- Line 11 is the number of model iterations. Multiplying the number of iterations by 10 will give the number of years in a model run.

- Line 12 is the random number seed. When this value is set to 0, LANDIS chooses a seed randomly. A valid number is any integer. Choosing a random number seed gives users control over the random number series and may help with model verification. The default value is 1.

- Line 13 is the length of the side of a map cell in meters. All LANDIS cells must be square (not rectangular). Recommended cell sizes are integers from 10 to 500 meters.

- Line 14 is the seed dispersal method identifier. Any identifier must be in upper case. The following identifiers are valid:

    NO_DISPERSAL—No seed movement at all.

    UNIFORM—All cells receive all seeds every iteration.

    NEIGHBORS—Each cell seeds its neighboring cell.

    DISPERSAL—Each cell seeds out to the species effective distance attribute. Within this distance species have a 95 percent chance of seeding out; beyond this distance species have a 5 percent chance of seeding out.

    RAND_ASYM—Each cell seeds in a random asymptotic manner for an infinite distance. This regime runs very slowly. Most runs will not complete in a reasonable amount of time.

    MAX_DIST—Each cell seeds out to the species maximum distance attribute.

    SIM_RAND_ASYM—Each cell seeds out to the species maximum distance attribute. Outside of this range cells have a small random chance of receiving seed of any species. This simulates the RAND_ASYM seeding regime but runs much faster.

- Lines 15-19 are entry file names (flags) for wind, fire, biological disturbance, fuel, and harvesting, respectively. If set to N/A, the particular disturbance or management will not be simulated. The use of these flags is described in the following chapters.

1 1 INPUT FILES

11.2 Species Attribute File (species.dat)

This file contains all of the life history attributes for every species in use. The maximum number of species allowed is 30. The species names are not fixed except for poputrem (trembling aspen) and popugran (big-tooth aspen). Species can be input in any order. However, because several other input files must use the same order, the order should not be changed once it is established.

The life history attributes are longevity, mature age, shade tolerance, fire tolerance, effective seeding distance, maximum seeding distance, vegetation propagation probability, maximum sprouting age, and reclassification coefficient. Species not present in the base year map can be omitted in the species attribute file. The following sample species attribute file was used in a LANDIS run for northern Wisconsin.

The set of attributes for each species is listed on a single line. Each of the nine data values in species.dat is described below:

#NAME	LONG	MTR	SHD	FIRE	EFFD	MAXD	VGP	SPAG	RCLC#
prunpenn	30	10	1	1	30	3000	0.0	10	0.25
poputrem	120	15	1	2	–1	–1	1.0	10	0.25
popugran	90	20	1	2	–1	–1	1.0	10	0.25
pinubank	90	15	1	2	20	40	0.0	0	0.25
pinuresi	250	35	2	4	12	275	0.0	0	0.75
querelli	300	35	2	5	30	3000	0.5	20	0.25
betupapy	120	30	2	2	200	5000	0.5	200	0.25
pinustro	450	15	3	3	100	250	0.0	0	1.00
acerrubr	150	10	3	1	100	200	0.5	20	0.50
querrubr	250	25	3	3	30	3000	0.5	20	0.75
piceglau	300	25	3	2	30	200	0.0	0	0.50
thujocci	400	30	4	1	45	60	0.5	20	0.50
fraxamer	150	30	4	1	70	140	0.1	20	0.75
betualle	350	40	4	2	100	400	0.1	20	0.75
tiliamer	250	15	4	2	30	120	0.5	20	0.75
abiebals	200	25	5	1	30	160	0.0	0	0.25
acersac2	400	40	5	1	100	200	0.1	20	0.75
tsugcana	640	30	5	3	30	100	0.0	0	1.00

11 INPUT FILES

LONG—Longevity of the species in years.

MTR—Maturity age of the species in years. The species will begin to seed when this age is reached.

SHD—Shade tolerance value (1-5). 1= least tolerant; 5= most tolerant.

FIRE—Fire tolerance value (1-5). The most fire-tolerant species are fire tolerance 5 while the least fire-tolerant species are fire tolerance 1.

EFFD—Species effective distance seeding range in meters. Within this distance species have a 95 percent chance of seeding out; beyond this distance species have a 5 percent chance of seeding out. –1 represents unlimited effective seeding range.

MAXD—Species maximum distance seeding range in meters. –1 represents unlimited maximum seeding range.

VGP—Probability of vegetative propagation following disturbance. It is specific to resprouting, not other types of reproduction such as root suckering.

SPAG—Maximum age to be able to resprout (vegetative propagation). The maximum age of resprouting is not currently implemented.

RCLC—Reclassification coefficient (0-1). This number is used in the output reclassification algorithm (see section 11.9). Functionally, these values are used to weight the classification of cells in output maps created by LANDIS. It can be considered as the theoretical importance coefficient of a species in comparison with other species. 0 is least important and 1 is most important.

11.3 Land Type Attribute File (landtype.dat)

A successful LANDIS run requires land type data reflecting differential species establishment among land types. To achieve this, a synthetic land type or ecoregion coverage is created from abiotic data layers such as climate, soil, geology, and topography. The land type attribute file contains the descriptions of each land type class in a LANDIS compatible format. LANDIS assumes that species may behave differently on different land types by having their own establishment coefficients (or reproduction probabilities). This assumption is supported by numerous experimental and empirical studies (He and Mladenoff 1999a). These coefficients must be developed for each land type and scaled from 0.00 to 1.00 (He *et al.* 1999b).

Land types are generally divided into two categories, active and nonactive. In LANDIS 4.0, nonactive land types are not processed by the model although they will be represented in output maps as their respective types. The current version includes empty, water, wetland, bog, lowland, and nonforest as the nonactive land types. The empty land type denotes any pixel outside the extent of the map. Active land types are any other land types. If the user needs to simulate fires on a lowland type, a land type name other than "lowland" can be used in the land type attribute file. The total number of land types should not exceed 65,536, as limited by the 16-bit ERDAS GIS map. The following is a sample land type attribute file.

```
moraine 40 700
  #prunpenn#        1
  #poputrem#        0.8
  #popugran#        1
  #pinubank#        0.5
  #pinuresi#        1
  #querelli#        0.5
  #betupapy#        1
  #pinustro#        1
  #acerrubr#        1
  #querrubr#        1
  #piceglau#        0.5
  #thujocci#        0
  #fraxamer#        0.3
  #betualle#        0.5
  #tiliamer#        0.8
  #abiebals#        0.3
  #acersac2#        0.5
  #tsugcana#        0.1
```

```
outwash 40 700
#prunpenn#        1
#poputrem#        0.3
#popugran#        0.5
#pinubank#        1
#pinuresi#        0.8
#querelli#        1
#betupapy#        0.3
#pinustro#        0.8
#acerrubr#        0.5
#querrubr#        0.5
#piceglau#        0.3
#thujocci#        0
#fraxamer#        0
#betualle#        0
#tiliamer#        0
#abiebals#        0
#acersac2#        0
#tsugcana#        0
```

In this example, there are two land types in total. Each land type is grouped together with one empty line in between. The first line contains three variables:

- The first identifier is the land type name. This name is case sensitive.

- The second variable represents the minimum age of cohort growth required before enough shade is created so that a shade tolerance 5 species can seed into the site on this land type. For instance, in order for a shade tolerance class 5 species such as balsam fir (abiebals), sugar maple (acersac2), or eastern hemlock (tsugcana) to seed into an outwash site, at least one other species must be present in an age class older than 40.

- The third variable is the initial time since last wind disturbance associated with all cells in the land type. This can be retrieved from disturbance history maps (if available). If adequate data are not available, we recommend using half the wind return interval for this variable. This can be set without requiring GIS processing.

- The next X lines where X equals the number of species modeled, are the species name in comments and their establishment coefficients (SEC) on the land type. The species order should be exactly the same as it is in the species attribute file.

Environmental changes encapsulated by land type can be incorporated in model simulations by specifying the "-e" argument followed by the year of interpolation. The land type attribute files must be derived per iteration. For example, if the land type attribute file name at year 0 is *LT*, the land type attribute file at year 10 should be *LT10*, at year 20 *LT20*, and so on, and each new land type attribute file will have different species establishment coefficients reflecting the environmental changes.

11.4 Land Type Map File (landtype.gis)

The land type input map is processed from several environmental data layers such as climate, soil, and topography. There are many ways to create the map using GIS. The final map file should be an ERDAS 7.4 8-bit or 16-bit GIS file. The model does not currently accept 4-bit GIS files. Within the GIS file, a continuous range of integers beginning from 0 should be used to represent the final overlaid map classes. For example, if the land type map contains 50 classes, 0 will represent the first class and 49 will represent the 50th class. A land type map class can represent any land type a user may wish to define. For example, 1 may represent a class of water land type with no species present; 10 may represent a class of moraine land type. Thus each integer corresponds to a class description in the land type attribute file (described above). The final class number can be as large as 65,536.

11.5 Species Composition Map File (speciesMap.gis)

The species composition map consists of species and species age classes. In many cases a species age map is not available for the study region. Interpolation of age information from other sources, such as the Forest Inventory and Analysis (FIA) database, can be used (He *et al.* 1998).

As with the land type map file, the forest composition map should be an ERDAS 7.4 8- or 16-bit GIS file. Within the GIS file, a continuous range of integers beginning from 0 should be used to represent the final overlaid map classes. If the map has 200 classes, 0 will represent the first class and 199 will represent the 200th class. For example, pixel value 10 may represent a class with hemlock, yellow birch, and sugar maple present and hemlock in the ages of 150, 200, 250, yellow birch in the ages of 80, 90, 100, and sugar maple in the ages of 30, 50, 150, 200. Each integer corresponds to a class description in the map attribute file (described below). Note that 0 should represent areas without data if such area exists, which will not be simulated. The final class number can be as large as 65,536.

11.6 Map Attribute File (mapAttribute.dat)

The map attribute file contains information about each of the classes present in the species composition map described above. The class descriptions are listed in sequential order where the first entry describes class 0 in the map file, the second entry describes class 1, and so forth. Any class in the map file should be represented in the map attribute file. The following is a sample map attribute file.

```
#class 0#
#prunpenn#     0  000
#poputrem#     0  000000000000
#popugran#     0  000000000
#pinubank#     0  000000000
#pinuresi#     0  00000000000000000000000000
#querelli#     0  000000000000000000000000000000
#betupapy#     0  000000000000
#pinustro#     0  0000000000000000000000000000000000000000000000000
#acerrubr#     0  000000000000000
#querrubr#     0  00000000000000000000000000
#piceglau#     0  000000000000000000000000000000
#thujocci#     0  000000000000000000000000000000000000
#fraxamer#     0  000000000000000
#betualle#     0  00000000000010000000000000000000000
#tiliamer#     0  00000000000000000000000
#abiebals#     0  00000000000000000000
#acersac2#     0  0000000000000000000000000000000000000000
#tsugcana#     0  0000000000000000000000000000000000000000000000000000000
```

```
#class 1#
#prunpenn#      0  000
#poputrem#      0  000000000000
#popugran#      0  000000000
#pinubank#      0  000000000
#pinuresi#      0  00000000000000000000000000000
#querelli#      0  000000000000000000000000000000000
#betupapy#      0  000001000000
#pinustro#      0  00000000000000001000000000000000000000000000000
#acerrubr#      0  000000000000000
#querrubr#      0  00000000000000000000000000
#piceglau#      0  00000000000000000000000000000000
#thujocci#      0  00000000100000001000000000000000000000000
#fraxamer#      1  000000000000000
#betualle#      0  0000000000001000000000000000000000000
#tiliamer#      0  0000000000000000000000000
#abiebals#      1  11100101110000000000
#acersac2#      0  10011011011000000000000000000000000000000
#tsugcana#      0  000000000001001000100000010000010100100001100000110000010
```

In the above example, class 0 is empty and class 1 is an old growth hemlock. The species should be listed in the same order as they appear in the species attributes file. Each species has two data elements associated with it: the first number is a vegetative propagation flag, and the numbers that follow represent an age list.

11 INPUT FILES

If a species has a 1 in the vegetative propagation flag, all cells of the cover type will be eligible for vegetative reproduction subject to the maximum age of resprouting and resprouting probability defined in the species attribute file.

Each column in the age list represents a 10-year cohort up to species longevity. A 0 denotes that the cohort is not present at that age class, while a 1 denotes the presence of that age class. For instance, abiebals has cohorts present at the 10, 20, 30, 60, 80, 90, and 100-year age classes. All class 2 cells within the forest composition map will be filled with the ages given above for abiebals at the beginning of a model run. In similar fashion, the other species with 1's listed in their age list will be present.

For class 1 in the above example, betupapy, pinustro, thujocci, betualle, abiebals, acersac2, and tsugcana are present on the site. Vegetative reproduction has been enabled for fraxamer and abiebals (note that fraxamer is not present).

11.7 Map Index File (mapIndex.dat)

Note: The map index file used to be called the reclassification output description file in earlier versions of LANDIS (LANDIS 2.0 -3.7).

LANDIS' internal data structures often contain more than 40MB of data depending on the map size. Since runs may be as long as 2,000 years, it may not be necessary to save out the complete internal state at each iteration. Instead, LANDIS attempts to create various maps (GIS files) using user-defined cover types by converting LANDIS' internal data format to user-defined thematic maps. This process is called output reclassification and is implemented through the map index file and the reclassification files (.RCS).

The map index file contains a list of names. Each name is used during the reclassification phase. Each name in the list consists of three or fewer characters, since for some operating systems the maximum file name allowed is still eight characters. An example map index file may look like this:

```
#mapindex.dat#
map oak std
```

After running LANDIS with this map index file you should find the following ERDAS 8-bit GIS files and their respective trailer files (TRL) in the output directory.

> map0.gis, map10.gis, ..., ..., map$n$.gis (n is the final simulation year)
>
> map0.trl, map10.trl, ..., ..., map$n$.gis
>
> oak0.gis, oak10.gis, ..., ..., oak$n$.gis
>
> oak0.trl, oak10.trl, ..., ..., oak$n$.trl
>
> std0.gis, std10.gis, ..., ..., std$n$.gis
>
> std0.trl, std10.trl, ..., ..., std$n$.trl

11.8 Reclassification File (RCS File)

For each name in the map index file there should be an associated RCS file. The RCS file specifies how to assign cover types for a given output map.

Using the map index file from the example in the last section, the user must provide three RCS files in the default directory: map.rcs, oak.rcs, and std.rcs. LANDIS searches for these files at run time. If any of these files are not present, output reclassification will not occur for the corresponding type.

Reclassification will reclassify maps based on the presence or absence of one or more species into a single, named GIS map. The method is effective and flexible. Users can examine single species or collections of species classified at different levels according to ecological principles. Continuing with our example may clarify the matter. "map.rsc," "oak.rcs," and "std.rcs" might look like this:

```
#map.rcs#
Maple:  acersac2
```

```
#oak.rcs#
Oak:  querelli querrubr
```

```
#std rcs#
Aspen:  prunpenn poputrem popugran !tsugcana !acersac2 !acerrubr
P_Birch:  betupapy !tsugcana !acersac2 !acerrubr
Maple:  acersac2 acerrubr !abiebals !tsugcana
Maple/Conifer:  acersac2 acerrubr abiebals !tsugcana
Hemlock:  tsugcana
Pine:  pinubank pinuresi pinustro !tsugcana
Y_Birch:  betualle
Oak:  querelli querrubr
```

In the first case the output map series map$n$.gis will contain acersac2. In the second case the *oak$n$.gis* series will contain both querelli and querrubr. The third case represents a more complicated situation. There are eight cover types defined: Aspen, P_Birch, Maple, Maple/Conifer, Hemlock, Pine, Y_Birch, and Oak.

The name denoting each cover type is defined by the user and is saved in each TRL file. Each name must be followed by a colon and then a list of one or more species names on the same line. There is no limit to the number of species in the list.

Each species following the cover type name is characteristic of the cover type unless the species name is preceded by an exclamation point. These species are not characteristic of the cover type. Presence of a noncharacteristic species will have a negative impact upon the likelihood of a cell being represented as the corresponding cover type. A fuzzy-logic-based algorithm determines which defined cover type most closely represents the current state.

11.9 Reclassification Algorithm

Some of the output reclassification algorithms are straightforward and not described here. These include the land type maps, the fire and wind maps, and the age maps.

The generic reclassification algorithm implementing the .RCS files is not nearly as straightforward. It can be summarized as follows.

```
For each site:
    For each species s:
        Determine dominance fuzzy value d(s).
    End For.
    Determine fuzzy reclassification vector v.
    Output correct reclassification class dependent on decision boundary within v.
End For.
```

The dominance fuzzy value is found by the following formula:

$$d(s) = \text{actual age of } s \text{ / maximum age of } s * \text{reclassification coefficient of } s.$$

The fuzzy reclassification vector v may be found by the following procedure:

```
For i=1 to n (where n is size of reclassification vector v).
    For each species s:
        If s is a positive influence on v(i)
            v(i)=v(i)+d(s)
        Else if s is a negative influence on v(i)
            v(i)=v(i)–d(s)
    End For
End For
```

The greatest value in vector $v(1), v(2), ..., v(n)$ will be the correct reclassification class. Note that in the above equations all mathematics are confined to fuzzy set rules. Thus all numbers are bounded in the range [0..1] and the result of any equation may never exceed 1 or be less than 0. If a number exceeds 1, it will be set to 1. If a number is less than 0, it will be set to 0.

11.10 Age Map Index File (ageIndex.dat)

Sometimes it is desirable to trace the dynamics of one or more species throughout the simulation run. The age map index file allows users to do just that. The age index file contains a list of names. Each name is used during the map output phase for each iteration. Each name in the list consists of three or fewer characters. A sample age map index file might look like the following:

```
#ageindex.dat#
ySM  yRO  yQA
```

After the model simulation using this age map index file, you should find the following ERDAS 8-bit GIS and TRL files in the output directory. The definition of each age map (e.g., ySM, yRO, and yQA) is discussed in the next section.

> ySM0.gis, ySM10.gis, ..., ..., ySM*n*.gis (*n* is the final year)
> ySM0.trl, ySM10.trl, ..., ..., ySM*n*.trl
> yRO0.gis, yRO10.gis, ..., ..., yRO*n*.gis
> yRO0.trl, yRO10.trl, ..., ..., yRO*n*.trl
> yQA0.gis, yQA10.gis, ..., ..., yQA*n*.gis
> yQA0.trl, yQA10.trl, ..., ..., yQA*n*.trl

11.11 Age File (.age)

For each name in the age map index file there should be an associated AGE file. The age file specifies which species to create age maps for. Using the age map index file from the example in the last section the user must provide three AGE files in the default directory: ySM.age , yRO.age , and yQA.age. LANDIS searches for these files at runtime. If any of these files are not present, output maps will not be created for the corresponding species. Example age files might look like the following:

```
#ySM.age#
  acersac2
```

```
#yRO.age#
  querrubr
```

```
#yQA.age#
  Poputrem
```

As shown above, each AGE file contains the name of an individual species and the name of the species is defined in species attribute file (species.dat).

11.12 Frequency File (frequency.dat)

The output generated by LANDIS defaults to every iteration (a 10-year time step). If this is not desired, the LANDIS output frequency file can be modified to affect the output intervals. Users can set their preferred output interval to something other than every iteration. This feature is useful when disk space is a concern. The format of the frequency file is as follows:

```
#LANDIS output frequency file::freq.dat#
#map indexed and age indexed species output interval# 1
#fire map output interval# 1
#wind map output interval# 1
#harvesting map output interval# 1
#30 year group age map output interval# 1
```

When the value specified falls in the range of 1 to 9, it is interpreted as a cyclic increment. Specifying 4, for instance, results in maps being output every fourth iteration (40 years). Specifying 0 or negative value results in no output for the category. When the value specified is greater than 9, it is interpreted as a single specific iteration. Specifying 50, for instance, results in maps being output on the 50th iteration (500th year). The above example outputs each iteration. Since LANDIS fire, wind, BDA, fuel, and harvesting modules incorporate stochastic algorithms, the time step of a disturbance event cannot be predicted until it occurs at a certain year. Thus, alternative map output does not apply, since it may omit the stochastic events. Currently, LANDIS 4.0 outputs disturbance maps every iteration regardless of the number specified in the output frequency file.

12. LANDIS WIND MODULE

The wind disturbance entry file (windInit.dat) is the only file needed by the LANDIS 4.0 wind module. Wind regimes are not differentiated by land types, so only a single prevailing wind regime can be defined and simulated in the LANDIS 4.0 WIND module. If windInit.dat or other wind entry file name is set in the LANDIS parameter file, wind disturbance will be simulated. The following is a sample of a wind disturbance entry file.

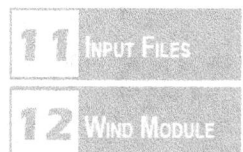

```
1            #1. standard wind disturbance mode#
900          #2. Minimum wind size.#
200000       #3. Maximum wind size.#
10000        #4. Mean wind size.#
800          #5. Mean return interval. changed from 1500 to 1000#
0.1          #6. Wind breakout coefficient#
2000         #7. Wind probability coefficient was 10#
1000         #8. Wind size coefficient was 50#
5            #9. Lower percentage of pseudomean#
10           #10. Upper percentage of pseudomean#
10           #11. pseudostrong#
5            #12. pseudolight#
wind         #13. Yearly output file.#
windfin      #14. Final output file.#
wind.log     #15. Wind log file.#
```

- The first variable is standard wind disturbance mode. Other disturbance modes are not available at this time.

- The second variable is the minimum wind size in square meters.

- The third variable is the maximum wind size in square meters.

- The fourth variable is the mean wind size in square meters. Over the course of a long model run (several thousand years) the mean wind size should be accurately simulated.

- The fifth variable is the mean wind return interval or wind disturbance cycle. This is the average years for wind to disturb all sites during the model run.

- The sixth variable is a wind breakout coefficient, the percent number of cells of the study area having wind events per decade. It ranges from 0.0 to 1.0, with 0.0 indicating that no cell is checked for breakout and 1.0 indicating that all cells are checked for possible wind occurrence.

- The seventh variable is wind probability coefficient. Probability coefficients can be adjusted interactively so that results match the predetermined mean return intervals. We recommend varying the probability coefficient by 10 each run. For example, if simulated wind disturbances happened more frequently than the predetermined mean return intervals, increase the probability coefficient by 10 each time. If fewer disturbances than expected happened, decrease the number by 10 each time. The scale of adjustment also depends on how different the simulated values are from the theoretical values.

- The eighth variable is wind size coefficient. When changing the value of the size coefficients for wind, we also recommend modifying it in increments of 10. For example, if simulated mean fire or wind disturbance size is less than the predetermined value in the disturbance file, increase the size coefficient by 10 each run. If the mean fire or wind disturbance size is greater than the predetermined value in the disturbance file, decrease the size coefficient by 10 each run. The size of the total adjustment will depend on how much the simulated values and the theoretical values differ.

- The following variables (9-12) are for the ratio mode disturbance modes (see LANDIS 3.7 Users Guide). They are no longer used, but need to be set as dummy numbers.

- Lines 13 to 15 contain file-naming information. The first name is the base for the name of the GIS map file for each 10-year time step or the step specified in *freq_out.put*. The year will be appended to the base. The GIS file will contain a visual representation of the wind damage for the current time step. The second name is the name of the final GIS file. This GIS file will contain a visual representation of the wind damage accumulated during the entire model run. The third name is the name of an ASCII text file that holds a record of all wind disturbances occurring in the model run.

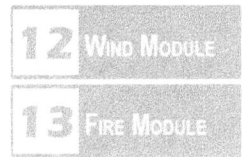

13. LANDIS FIRE MODULE

13.1 Fire Entry File (fireParameter.dat)

If fireParameter.dat or other fire entry file name is set in the LANDIS parameter file, the fire module will be activated. The following is a sample of fire entry file.

```
1                      #1. Flag of new fire algorithms incorporation#
1                      #2. Flag of wind incorporation#
1                      #3. Flag of using DEM data#
1                      #4. Flag of using independent fire regime data#
1                      #5. Flag of output TSLF#
0.1 0.2 0.3 0.4 0.5    #6. fire initiation probability for each fine fuel class#
0.300000               #7. Base probability for fuel class 3#
0.200000               #8. Wind coefficient#
0.000000               #9. Topography coefficient#
1.000000               #10. Predefined fire size distribution coefficient#
30                     #11. Percentage (%) of nonwind events in wind regime#
10 15 20 25 30         #12. Cumulative probabilities for SW direction wind with
                           intensity class 1 to 5#
```

```
30  30  35  40  40      #13. Cumulative probabilities for W direction wind with
                        intensity class 1 to 5#
40  40  40  40  40      #14. Cumulative probabilities for NW direction wind with
                        intensity class 1 to 5#
45  50  55  60  60      #15. Cumulative probabilities for N direction wind with
                        intensity class 1 to 5#
60  60  60  60  60      #16. Cumulative probabilities for NE direction wind with
                        intensity class 1 to 5#
60  60  60  60  60      #17. Cumulative probabilities for E direction wind with
                        intensity class 1 to 5#
65  70  75  75  75      #18. Cumulative probabilities for SE direction wind with
                        intensity class 1 to 5#
80  85  90  95  100     #19. Cumulative probabilities for S direction wind with
                        intensity class 1 to 5#
fireRegimeAttr.dat      #20. Fire regime attribute input file#
fireRegimeData.gis      #21. Fire regime GIS input data file#
DEM500.dat              #22. Landscape elevation ASCII input data file#
Fire                    #23. File name used to output fire map each iteration#
Firefin                 #24. Final output file#
Fire.log                #25. Fire log file#
30                      #26. Cell size. Unit: meters#
```

- If the Using-New-Fire-Algorithm-Flag (line 1) is set to 1, the fire module will use fine fuel to simulate fire initiation if the fuel module is also turned on, or use TSLF (Time Since Last Fire algorithm) to calculate fire initiation probability when fuel module is off. The fire module will also use the new fire spread algorithm, which incorporates wind, topography, fuel, and fire size distribution. The fire module will use fuel class provided by fuel module to determine fire intensity when the fuel module is also on, or use TSLF when the fuel module is off. If the flag is set to 0, the fire module will use TSLF to simulate fire initiation and fire intensity, and use the old fire spread algorithm from LANDIS 3.7 that does not contain capabilities to simulate the effects of terrain, wind regime, and fuel.

- If the Wind-Incorporation-Flag (line 2) is set to 0, the fire module will not simulate effects of wind on fire spread, even if wind coefficient (line 8) is non-zero. To simulate wind effects on fire spread, both the Using-New-Fire-Algorithm-Flag and Wind-Incorporation-Flag must be set to 1.

- If the Using-DEM-Flag (line 3) is set to 1, the fire module will try to read DEM data (line 22) and use it when the Using-New-Fire-Algorithm-Flag is also on.

- If the Using-Independent-Fire-Regime-Flag (line 4) is set to 1, the fire module will read fire regime GIS file (line 21). Otherwise, it will use the land type map.

- If the Output-TSLF-Flag (line 5) is set to 1, the fire module will output time since last fire map. The file name is fixed: TSLF0.gis is the initial time-since-last-fire GIS map; TSLF1.gis is the time-since-last-fire GIS map after the first iteration simulation, etc.

- Fire initiation probability for each fine fuel class 1 to 5 is set in line 6. Each value ranges from 0 to 1. Fine fuel class of a site is dependent on species/age composition of the site, and this composition mainly determines whether or not an ignition can initiate a fire. Since it is simulated by a Bernoulli function with the probability specified here, the probability indicates the proportion of fire ignitions that become fires given each fine fuel class. For example, given an initiation probability in fuel class 1 of 0.1, if there are 100 ignitions simulated in an area with fine fuel class 1, there will be about 100 * 0.1 = 10 fire occurrences.

- Base probability (line 7) is used in the new fire spread algorithm when the fuel module is on. This probability will be the fire spread probability of fuel class (potential fire intensity class in fuel module) 3. A preliminary sensitivity analysis has shown that fire spread probability has a nonlinear effect on the burned patch size and the critical probability is around 0.29. That is to say, for a homogeneous landscape where all sites have fuel class 3, fire will spread across the landscape if the base probability is above 0.29 provided there are no other effects (i.e., wind, topography, predefined fire size distribution) taken into account.

- Wind coefficient (line 8) is used to weight the effects of wind on fire spread probability. The range of this coefficient is 0 to 2. Please refer to fire spread probability equation in fire module design for details (section 7.5.2.2). Increasing the wind coefficient will increase the fire spread probability in the wind direction. If the wind coefficient is 0, there will be no effects on fire spread probability.

- Topography coefficient (line 9) is used to weight the terrain effects on fire spread probability. The range of this coefficient is 0 to 2. Please refer to fire spread probability equation in fire module design for details (section 7.5.2.2). If the topography coefficient is 0, there will be no topographic effects on spread probability. Otherwise, an uphill slope will increase the spread probability, and the magnitude of such increase is decided by the slope angle and topography coefficient. If the landscape is flat, the topography coefficient should be a little higher (above 0.5) to simulate topographical effects. However, in a mountainous landscape, the coefficient should be smaller (under 0.5) to avoid unrealistic simulation of the effects of topography on fire spread behavior.

- Predefined fire size distribution coefficient (line 10) is used to weight the effects of fire size distribution on fire spread. The range of this coefficient is 0 to 2. Please refer to fire spread probability equation in fire module design for details (section 7.5.2.2). If this coefficient is set to 0, the predefined fire size distribution will have no effect on the fire spread simulation, and only fuel, wind, and topography will decide fire size and spread behavior. Therefore, if the users intend to have the fire regime observe the fire size distribution described by mean fire size and standard deviation, the coefficient should be towards the high end (above 1).

- Line 11 defines the percentage of nonwind events that are simulated in one iteration, when both the Using-New-Fire-Algorithm-Flag (line 1) and Wind-Incorporation-Flag (line 2) are turned on. The range is 0 to 100. In the example data, the value is 30, which means 30 percent of simulated fire events in one iteration will not have wind events simulated.

- Line 12 to line 19 set the cumulative probabilities of all 40 wind event classes. There are eight directions and each direction has five wind intensity classes. Each line represents one direction. They are SW, W, NW, N, NE, E, SE, and S sequentially. The values on each line are the cumulative probabilities for each of the five wind intensity classes in that wind direction, and the probabilities are cumulative over all 40 classes. The

13 FIRE MODULE

range of each value is 0 to 100. Notice that the prior value must be less than or equal to the following value and the last of the 40 numbers must be 100 to observe cumulative probability rules. From the example data, line 12 indicates that the percentages of SW wind with intensity class 1, 2, 3, 4, and 5 are 10 percent, 5 percent (10-15), 5 percent (15-20), 5 percent (20-25), and 5 percent (25-30), respectively. Line 14 indicates that there are no NW winds in any intensity class since the cumulative probabilities do not change.

- Line 20 and line 21 specify the name of fire regime attribute data file and the associated fire regime map file.

- Line 22 specifies the name of the DEM data file. The DEM file must be an ASCII file containing height information for each cell in meters.

- Line 23, line 24, and line 25 specify file names used for fire output. The names are used for the simulated fire intensity map at each time step, the final cumulative fire intensity map, and the log of each simulated fire event, respectively.

- Line 26 specifies the cell size of the maps (meters), which must be consistent with that specified in the LANDIS parameter file.

Figure 11 shows how different flags and the fuel module control the flow of the simulation by the fire module.

13.2 Fire Regime Attribute File (fireRegimeAttr.dat)

The fire regime attribute file specifies the attributes of each fire regime unit for the fire module. The first fire regime unit that appears in the fire regime attribute file is coded 0 in the fire regime map (e.g., fireRegimeData.gis) when Using-Independent-Fire-Regime-Flag is 1 or in the land type map (e.g., landType.gis) when Using-Independent-Fire-Regime-Flag is 0. Similarly, the second fire regime unit that appears in the fire regime attribute file is coded 1 in the fire regime map or in the land type map, and so on. For each fire regime unit, a set of properties will be described in a fixed order, as the following example shows:

```
swslope                #1. Fire regime name#
415                    #2. Mean fire return interval#
0.1                    #3. Fire ignition density#
4.5                    #4. MFS, unit: hectare#
1.8                    #5. STD#
50                     #6. Last fire disturbance#
10 60 90 120 150       #7. fire curve, time since last fire#
1 2 3 4 5              #8. fire intensity classes#
10 20 60 80 100        #9. wind curve, time since last wind#
1 2 3 3 3              #10. modified fire classes#
```

- Line 1 is the name of the fire regime. It does not have to be the same as the name of the land type. The name is case sensitive.

- Line 2 specifies the mean fire return interval (i.e., fire cycle) of the fire regime. The unit is years.

- Line 3 is ignition density (i.e., ignition rate) of the fire regime. The unit is #per decade per hectare.

- Line 4 and line 5 specify two statistics of the fire size distribution of the fire regime (mean and standard deviation of fire size). The unit is hectares.

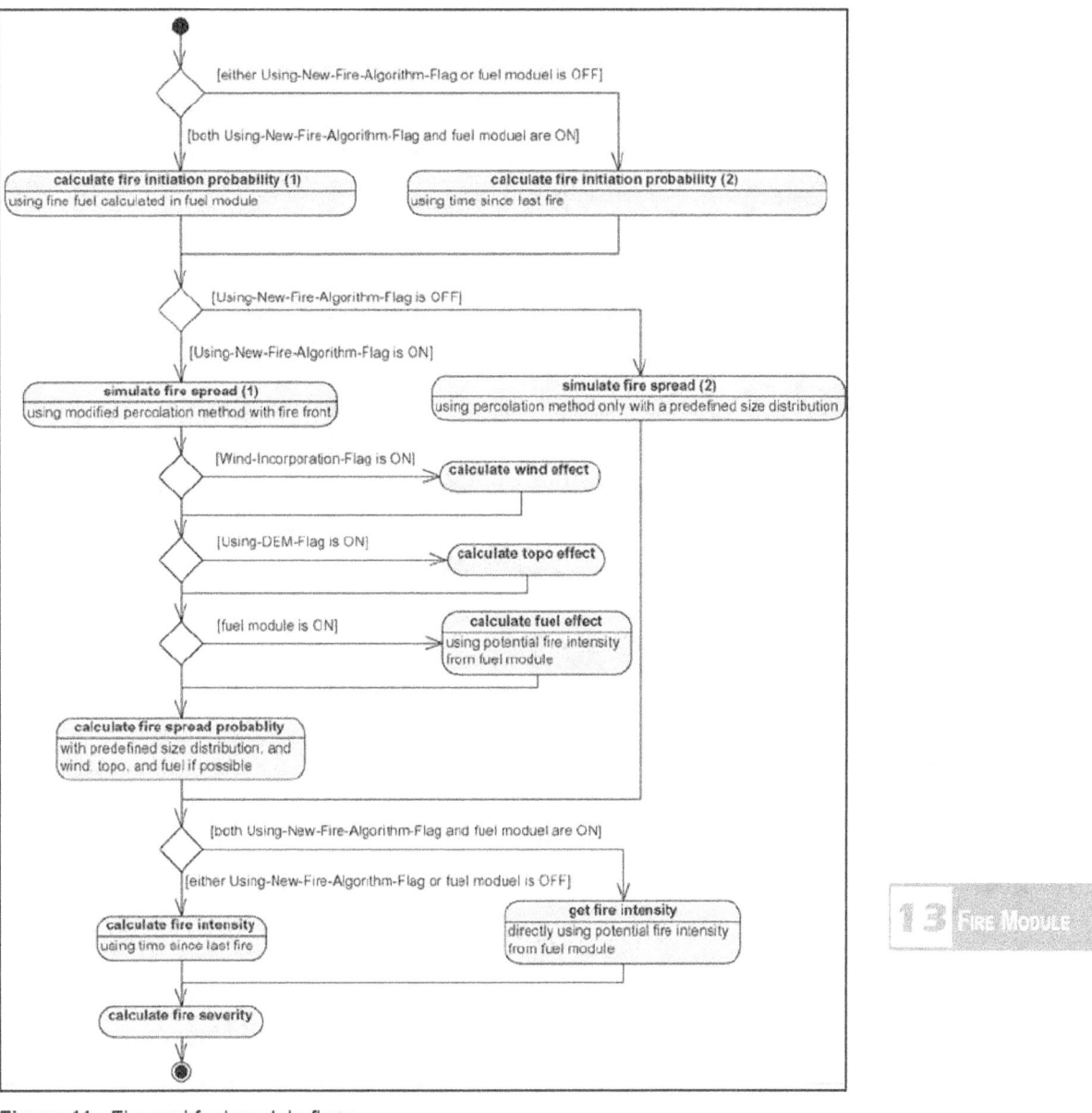

Figure 11. Fire and fuel module flags.

- Line 6 is the time since last fire that is used as initial conditions for land under this fire regime. It is needed even when a land type map is used as fire regime input map.

- Lines 7, 8, 9, and 10 specify the fire curve, fire intensity class, wind curve, and modified fire intensity class, respectively. They are inherited from LANDIS 3.7 and used only when the fuel module is turned off. The fire curve represents the fuel accumulation processes, and fire intensity classes are respective fire intensity classes when time since last fire reaches a certain period as specified in the fire curve. For example, if the last fire occurred 50 years ago, the fire intensity class should be 1 since the curve in the example specifies that when time since last fire is between 10 and 50, the fire intensity class is 1 for this fire regime unit. Time since last wind and modified fire intensity classes (wind curve) are also used in the fire intensity calculation if wind module is turned on, and the final fire intensity class is the larger value between the two curves. In addition to this

example, if last wind also happened 50 years ago, since the modified fire
intensity class specified by the wind curve is 2, the final fire intensity class
will be 2, which is the larger of 1 and 2. When wind module is turned off,
these parameters are still required but will not be used. Note that LANDIS
4.0 fire module uses its own wind parameters (wind direction and intensity)
to simulate fire spread.

13.3 Fire regime and DEM maps

Fire regime map is an (optional) input for LANDIS 4.0 fire module and the
file (e.g., fireRegimeData.gis) is an ERDAS 7.4 8-bit or 16-bit GIS file. Within
the GIS file, a continuous range of integers beginning with 0 should be used to
represent the fire regime classes specified in the fire regime attribute file. For
example, if the fire regime map contains 50 classes, 0 will represent the first fire
regime and 49 will represent the 50th fire regime. Thus each integer corresponds
to a class description in the fire regime attribute file. The final class number can
be as large as 65,536.

A DEM map is also needed for the new LANDIS fire module if the Using-DEM-
Flag is set to 1. The file (e.g., DEM500.dat) must be an ASCII file containing
height information for each cell in meters. There are no header files or header
part needed for the DEM map. LANDIS assumes that the DEM map has the same
rows, columns, and cell size attributes as the other input ERDAS 7.4 GIS files.

14. LANDIS BDA MODULE

14.1 Entry File (BDAInit.dat)

If BDAInit.dat or other BDA entry file name is set in the LANDIS parameter file,
the BDA module will be activated. The following is an example of a BDA entry
file.

```
              2      #BDA number#
              0      #Neighbor speed up#
#BDA name 1#         budworm.dat
#BDA name 2#         beetle.dat
```

- The BDA number defines the number of different disturbance agents the
  BDA will simulate.

- The Neighborhood speed up flag determines whether the BDA module
  will use every cell in a neighborhood to calculate Neighborhood Resource
  Dominance (0), or use the subsampling procedure to calculate NRD (1).

- Each BDA simulated must have a corresponding BDA parameter file. The
  file names for each are defined here. Note that the number of file names
  must match the BDA number.

13 FIRE MODULE

14 BDA MODULE

14.2 BDA Parameter File

```
budworm              #1. BDA Name#
Budworm.gis          #2. Initial Conditions map#
1                    #3. BDP Calibrator#
mean                 #4. SRDMod#
10                   #5. time step (years)#
5                    #6. number of LTM#
Empty   -999         #7. Landtype Name##Modifier Value#
Water   -999         #8. Landtype Name##Modifier Value#
Xeric   0.16         #9. Landtype Name##Modifier Value#
Mesic   0.0          #10. Landtype Name##Modifier Value#
Hydric  -0.16        #11. Landtype Name##Modifier Value#
1                    #12. Number of Disturbance Modifiers#
Wind                 #13. Disturbance Type#
20                   #14. Modifier Duration (years)#
0.33                 #15. Disturbance Modifier Value#
20                   #16. TimeSinceLastEpidemic(years)#
cyclic               #17. TempPattern not used in new version#
pulse                #18. TempType: pulse, variablepulse, continuous#
RFnormal             #19. RandomFuncton: RFnormal or RFuniform#
25                   #20. Random Parameter 1#
10                   #21. Random Parameter 2#
10                   #22. TemporalFreq#
0                    #23. MinROS#
3                    #24. MaxROS#


5                    #26. number of species#
```

#Species Name#	Minor Host Age	Secondary Host Age	Primary Host Age	Susceptibility Class 3 Age	Susceptibility Class 2 Age	Susceptibility Class 1 Age
Abiebals	0	20	30	0	20	40
Betupapy	999	999	999	999	999	999
Piceglau	0	20	70	30	60	999
Picemari	20	60	999	20	60	999
Poputrem	999	999	999	999	999	999

```
1                    #34. NeighborhoodFlag#
1000                 #35. NeighborRadius (meters)#
uniform              #36. NeighborShape (uniform, linear, gaussian)#
10                   #37. NeighborWeight#


1                    #39. Dispersal Flag, not used#
1                    #40. Spatial##[1 = synchronous, 0 = asynchronous]#
100                  #41. DispersalRate (meters/year)#
0.3                  #42. EpidemicThresh#
5                    #43. InitialEpicenterNum#
0                    #44. SeedEpicenter#
0.01                 #45. outbreak epicenter coeff#
20                   #46. seed epicenter coeff#
none                 #47. InitialCondition: "map", "none"]#
0                    #48. Dispersal template#
```

14 BDA MODULE

- BDA name will define the name of the disturbance output, where the year of simulation and .gis extension are added to the corresponding Erdas output map. The BDA will automatically place all output in a BDA subfolder within the output folder defined in the parameter.dat file.

- Initial Conditions map is an optional map that may be used to characterize current outbreak activity for a BDA. This line for optional map is for future enhancement and is not currently used. Its purpose will be to provide site locations for current insect activity that may act as dispersal sites for future outbreaks. The format of the map will be an ERDAS 8-bit map with attributes identical to the BDA disturbance maps currently produced by the BDA module.

- BDP Calibrator represents the "*a*" parameter of equation 9 (section 9.5.5.5).

- Site Resources Dominance Mode may be set to either "max" or "mean."

- The time step is currently restricted by LANDIS 4.0 to be 10, but may be modified here for future variable time step versions of LANDIS.

- The number of Land Type Modifiers (i.e., line 6; LTM) must match the number of land types in the landtype.dat file. Lines 7-10 here represent the input for the LTMs. Each must have a name that corresponds with the landtype.dat file, and a real value from –1.0 to 1.0 that represents the land type influence on site resource dominance (see section 9.5.5.2). Note that a value of -999 indicates the land type will be ignored when calculating a neighborhood resource dominance value.

- Lines 12-16 represent the disturbance modifier parameters. For each disturbance that may modify the BDA (e.g., Wind, Fire, Harvest, or another BDA), three parameters are required: Disturbance Type, the duration of the modifying effect (in years), and the modifier value (between –1.0 to 1.0) for the first time step following the disturbance. Note that the disturbance modifier value represents the influence of a specific disturbance type on site resource dominance (see section 9.5.5.2) and is assumed to decline linearly with time since that disturbance for the duration of the modifying effect.

- Lines 16-24 represent the temporal parameters that control the landscape scale intensity of the BDA at a given time step, termed Regional Outbreak Status (ROS). ROS units are integer classes ranging from 0 (no outbreak) to 3 (intense outbreak).

  - *TimeSinceLastEpidemic* represents the time in years since the last outbreak.

  - *TempPattern* is an old parameter no longer used. A value is still required for this LANDIS version.

  - *TempType* valid inputs = pulse, variablepulse, and continuous. TempType determines whether outbreaks are binary (either MinROS or MaxROS—see definitions below; TempType = "pulse") or if the ROS can range between those values (TempType = "variable pulse"). Note that continuous temporal types are still under development and currently not operational.

  - *RandomFunction* represents the type of function used to control the pattern of outbreaks. Options are "RFnormal" for a normally distributed random function defined by a mean μ and standard deviation σ, and "RFuniform" for a uniformly distributed random function defined by a minimum interval (*MinI*) and a maximum value (*MaxI*).

14 BDA MODULE

- The definition of RandomParameter1 depends on the RandomFunction selected: μ if using *RFnormal*, or *MinI* if using *RFuniform*.

- The definition of RandomParameter2 also depends on the RandomFunction selected: σ if using *RFnormal*, or *MaxI* if using *RFuniform*.

- *TemporalFreq* is another old parameter no longer used. A value is still required for this LANDIS version.

- *MaxROS* = Maximum Outbreak Status; defines the maximum intensity of a regional outbreak. Parameter value must be an integer value between 1 (light outbreak) and 3 (intense outbreak).

- *MinROS* = Minimum Outbreak Status; defines the "background" outbreak activity that will occur in each time step. Parameter value must be an integer value between 0 (no outbreak) and 3 (intense outbreak). It can equal MaxROS, but cannot exceed it.

- Lines 26-32 represent tree species parameters.

  - The number of species must match the number of species in the species.dat file.

  - Each tree species must have a name that corresponds with a name in the species.dat file.

  - Minor, Secondary, and Primary Host Ages indicate the minimum age at which a species enters the respective Host Preference Class. These classes are used to calculate Site Resource Dominance (SRD). A value greater than the tree species longevity (e.g., 999) indicates that the species never reaches the indicated class.

  - Susceptibility Class Ages indicate the minimum age at which a species enters a respective tree species cohort susceptibility class. These classes determine the age class thresholds of biological disturbance probability (BDP) required to kill a species cohort if a site is disturbed. A value greater than the tree species longevity (e.g., 999) indicates that the species never reaches the indicated class. Cohorts younger than the minimum age for susceptibility class 3 are assigned a susceptibility class of 4 and are immune to the BDA.

- Lines 34-37 are Neighborhood Resource Dominance parameters.

  - NeighborhoodFlag determines whether NRD is used in calculating BDP.

  - NeighborhoodRadius defines the radius of the neighborhood influence in meters.

  - NeighborShape defines the radial function used to calculate NRD. Valid entries are: uniform, linear, or Gaussian.

  - NeighborWeight (NW) defines the importance of NRD relative to SRD when calculating BDP.

- Lines 39-48 are Dispersal parameters.

  - The DispersalFlag is not currently used, but an entry is still required for the current LANDIS version.

  - Spatial is a flag that determines whether dispersal is used. Here 1 = "spatially synchronous" (i.e., dispersal routines are NOT used), and 0 = "spatially asynchronous" (i.e., dispersal routines are used).

- DispersalRate defines the annual rate of dispersal in meters per year.

- EpidemicThresh defines the minimum BDP required for an Epicenter to be selected.

- InitialEpicenterNum defines the number of epicenters that will be selected at time = 0. This is typically used to initiate an outbreak(s) that will spread over the course of the simulation.

- SeedEpicenter is a flag that determines when new epicenters will "seed" new outbreaks outside of current outbreak zones.

- OutbreakEpicenterCoeff is the "c" parameter corresponding with Equation 10 (section 9.5.5.6.1) for epicenters that will start from within the outbreak zone that occurred at time = t–1.

- SeedEpicenterCoeff is the "c" parameter corresponding with Equation 10 for new epicenters that will start outside of the outbreak zone defined at time = t–1.

- InitialCondition specifies whether an input map is used to define known outbreaks at time = 0.

- DispersalTemplate defines the structuring element (i.e., the neighborhood rule) controlling the percolation of the BDA from an epicenter to its dispersal radius defined by DispersalRate×TimeStep. Numeric options are: 0 = regular dispersal (i.e., disperse to maximum radius); 1 = 4-neighbor structuring element; 2 = 8-neighbor structuring element; 3 = 12-neighbor structuring element; 4 = 24-neighbor structuring element.

15. LANDIS FUEL MODULE

15.1 Fuel Entry File (fuelInit.dat)

If fuelInit.dat or other fuel entry file name is set in the LANDIS parameter file, the fuel module will be activated and fuel status will be used by the fire module (see discussions under fire module for situations when fuel module is turned off). The following is an example of the fuel entry file.

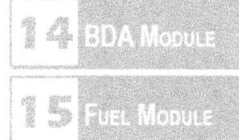

```
fuelinput.dat          #1. fuel module input file#
FuelRule.dat           #2. fuel module rules file#
fireRegimeAttr.dat     #3. Fire regime attributes#
fireRegimeData.gis     #4. Fire regime map#
fuelman.dat            #5. N/A or Fuel management event file#
fuel.log               #6. Fuel tracking output file#
fuelman.log            #7. Fuel management output file#
stand_fuel.log         #8. Fuel management output for each stand#
stand500.gis           #9. Stand identifier input map file#
ma_500.gis             #10. Management area identifier input map#
```

- Fuel module input file (line 1) contains parameters of fuel accumulation and decomposition by land type, as well as fuel modifiers including fire, wind, BDA, and harvest. See section 15.3.

- Fuel module rule file (line 2) contains user-defined rules for defining potential fire intensity based upon coarse fuel and fine fuel. See section 15.3.

- Fire regime attributes file (line 3) has fire regime parameters of LANDIS 3.7. Fire regime map (line 4) is the 8-bit ERDAS GIS map that defines various fire regimes. If fire module is turned on, these two files (fire regime attributes file and fire regime map) should be consistent with the files used in fire module. If the fire module is turned off, the user must provide these two files as they are both used in fuel module.

- Fuel management event file (line 5) contains a fuel management treatment prescription. If set to N/A, fuel management will not be simulated.

- Fuel log file (line 6) outputs some general information for each simulation year, e.g., fine fuel loads, coarse fuel loads, and potential fire risk. Detailed information can be found in section 15.3.

- Fuel management log file (line 7) logs all fuel treatments simulated based upon the treatment prescriptions by management area (or unit).

- Fuel stand log file (line 8) logs all fuel treatments simulated based upon the treatment prescriptions by stands.

- Line 9 and line 10 are 16-bit ERDAS input maps of stand and management area, respectively.

15.2 Fuel Module Input File (fuelInput.dat)

1	**[SPECIES]**					
	#Live fuel quality coefficient (FQC) by species#					
2	#Species 1#	0.2				
3	#Species 2#	0.8				
4	...	...				
5	#Species N#	0.6				
	#Fine fuel accumulation curves by species#					
	##					
6	#Fine fuel classes for species 1#	1	2	3	4	5
7	#Age of species 1#	0	20	50	110	180
8	#Fine fuel classes for species 2#	1	2	3	3	3
9	#Age of species 2#	20	60	140	200	240
10	#Fine fuel classes for species 3#	2	1	2	3	4
11	#Age of species 3#	10	30	60	110	180
12	...	...				
13	#Fine fuel classes for species N#	1	2	3	4	5
14	#Age of species N#	0	20	50	110	180
15	**[LANDTYPE]**					
	#Probability of low/medium intensity fire to become a crown fire#					
16	#Landtype 1#	0.02				
17	...	...				
18	#Landtype M#	0.15				
	#Landtype modifiers of fine fuel and coarse fuel#					
19	#Landtype name#	Landtype1				
	#Fine fuel classes#	#1	2	3	4	5#
20	#Fine fuel loads modified by landtype1#	1	1	2	3	4
	#Coarse fuel accumulation curve for landtype1#					
	#Coarse fuel classes#	#1	2	3	4	5#
21	#Years of coarse fuel accumulation to reach the corresponding classes#	20	60	110	170	220
	#Coarse fuel decomposition curve for landtype1#					
	#Coarse fuel classes#	#4	3	2	1	0#

15 FUEL MODULE

22	#Years of decomposition					
	since last disturbance#	20	60	100	140	20
23	...	...				
24	#Landtype name#	LandtypeN				
	#Fine fuel classes#	#1	2	3	4	5#
25	#Fine fuel loads modified by landtypeN#	2	3	4	5	5
	#Coarse fuel accumulation curve for landtypeN#					
	#Coarse fuel classes#	#1	2	3	4	5#
26	#Years of coarse fuel accumulation					
	to reach the corresponding classes#	30	100	250	600	700
	#Coarse fuel decomposition curve for landtypeN#					
	#Coarse fuel classes#	#4	3	2	1	0#
27	#Years of decomposition					
	since last disturbance#	10	50	80	120	160
28	**[FIRE]**					
	#Fire intensity classes#	#1	2	3	4	5#
29	#Fine fuel reduction#	−1	−2	−3	−3	−3
30	#Coarse fuel reduction#	0	−1	−2	−3	−3
31	**[WIND]**					
	#Wind intensity classes#	#1	2	3	4	5#
32	#number of fine fuel classes increased#	1	1	2	2	3
33	#number of coarse fuel classes increased#	1	2	3	4	4
34	**[BDA]**					
35	#Total BDA types#	2				
	#BDA type 1#					
	#BDA intensity classes#	#1	2	3#		
36	#number of fine fuel classes increased#	1	1	2		
37	#number of coarse fuel classes increased#	1	2	3		
	#BDA type 2#					
	#BDA intensity classes#	#1	2	3#		
38	#number of fine fuel classes increased#	0	1	2		
39	#number of coarse fuel classes increased#	1	2	2		
40	**[HARVEST]**					
41	#Total harvest events#	2				
	#Harvest event 1#					
	#Fine fuel load before harvest#	#0	1	2	3	4	5#
42	#Fine fuel load after harvest#	2	2	3	4	5	5
	#Coarse fuel load before harvest#	#0	1	2	3	4	5#
43	#Coarse fuel load after harvest#	2	3	3	4	5	5
	#Harvest event 2#					
	#Fine fuel load before harvest#	#0	1	2	3	4	5#
44	#Fine fuel load after harvest#	1	2	3	4	5	5#
	#Coarse fuel load before harvest#	#0	1	2	3	4	5#
45	#Coarse fuel load after harvest#	1	2	3	4	5	5

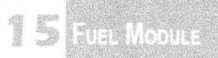
15 FUEL MODULE

Species section

- The species section begins with a string named "[SPECIES]" (line 1). The name is specified and upper case is required.

- Fuel quality coefficient (FQC) (lines 2-5). Fuel from different species may have different flammability due to differences in physical and chemical attributes (Brown *et al.* 1982). We use a fuel quality coefficient (0<FQC<=1) to summarize such differences on a relative scale. Species with low FQC are less flammable than species with high FQC. FQCs are ranked and parameterized by users, and the same value (e.g., FQC=1) can be used for all species if there are no discernible differences among species.

- Fine fuel accumulation curve (lines 6-14). Fine fuel accumulation curve is defined for each species and depicts the relationship between fine fuel production and species age. For some species (e. g., species 1, lines 6-7), the fine fuel loads may accumulate up to class 5 when this species reaches its longevity. Other species may not accumulate to such a level. For example, in species 2 (lines 8-9), the fine fuel load can only accumulate to class 3. Fine fuel accumulation curves can have multiple peaks (e.g., lines 10-11) and do not have to follow an ascending order. However, the data line of tree age must follow the ascending order, and only five values can be set for each line.

Land type section

- The land type section begins with a string named "[LANDTYPE]" (line 15). The name is specified and upper case is required.

- The probability that low/medium fire class will become crown fire by land type (lines 16-18). Because of the existence of live fuels, a fire may jump from surface fire to a crown fire, and this probability may vary differently among land types. Lines 16-18 define this probability (P) for each land type.

- Land type name (line 19). This gives the name of each land type. The name and the order of each land type should be consistent with that in land type attribute file (landtype.dat).

- Fine fuel modifier (line 20). Fine fuel decomposition rates may vary by land types. Thus, a land type modifier may decrease or increase the fine fuel class derived from species age cohorts. For example, a fine fuel class 3 on a mesic land type might decrease to class 2 because the decomposition rate is relatively high, while the same fuel class (3) on a xeric land type might increase to class 4, since the decomposition rate is relatively low. The user defines the modifier in the land type parameter file, and the default is no modification.

- Curve of coarse fuel accumulation (line 21). Stand age (the oldest age cohorts) in combination with disturbance history (time since last disturbance) are used to determine the coarse fuel accumulation. In the absence of disturbance, the accumulation process dominates until the amount of coarse fuel reaches a level where decomposition and accumulation are in balance. The curve of coarse fuel accumulation describes the relation of coarse fuel loading as a function of accumulation year, in the absence of disturbance. In this example, the coarse fuel load will accumulate to class 1 after 20 years of accumulation, class 2 after 60 years, class 3 after 110 years, class 4 after 170 years, and class 5 after 220 years.

- Curve of coarse fuel decomposition (line 22). Disturbances, e.g., wind, insect and disease, and harvest, can cause tree mortality and increase coarse fuel. The increased coarse fuel will decompose and the decomposition rate varies by land types. In this example, when additional coarse fuels are added by disturbance, the coarse fuels will gradually decompose from class 5 to class 4 in 20 years, to class 3 in 60 years, to class 2 in 100 years, to class 1 in 140 years, and to class 0 in 200 years. However, coarse fuels will rarely reach the very low classes (e.g. 0) because coarse fuels also accumulate through time.

15 FUEL MODULE

- Lines 23-27 give the input of all other land types, which repeat the information in lines 19-22.

Fire section

- Fire modifier Section (line 28). This section begins with a string named "[FIRE]". The name is specified and upper case is required. This section and all the inputs under this section are required, whether the fire module is turned on or off. If the fire module is turned on, the fire modifier can have effects on fuel loading. Otherwise, this information will be ignored.
- Fire modifier on fine fuel (line 29). This line defines the fine fuel reduction by each fire intensity class.
- Fire modifier on coarse fuel (line 30). This line defines the coarse fuel reduction or increase by each fire intensity class.

Wind section

- Wind Section (line 31). This section begins with a string named "[WIND]". The name is specified and upper case is required. This section and all the inputs under this section are required, whether the wind module is turned on or off. If the wind module is turned on, the wind modifier can have effects on fuel loading. Otherwise, this information will be ignored.
- Wind modifier on fine fuel (line 32). This line defines the fine fuel increase by each wind intensity class.
- Wind modifier on coarse fuel (line 33). This line defines the coarse fuel increase by each wind intensity class.

BDA section

- BDA modifier Section (line 34). This section begins with a string named "[BDA]". The name is specified and upper case is required. This section and all the inputs under this section are required, whether the BDA module is turned on or off. If BDA module is turned on, the BDA modifier may have effects on fuel loading. Otherwise, this information will be ignored.
- Total BDA types (line 35). This gives the total number of BDA types. This number should be consistent with the number defined in BDA attribute files.

- BDA modifier on fine fuel (line 36). This line defines the fine fuel increase/ decrease by each BDA intensity class for BDA type 1.
- BDA modifier on coarse fuel (line 37). This line defines the coarse fuel reduction/increase by each BDA intensity class for BDA type 1.
- BDA modifier on fine fuel (line 38). This line defines the fine fuel increase/ decrease based on the BDA intensity class for BDA type 2. If there are more than two BDA types, the modifiers for each BDA should be input sequentially by BDA.
- BDA modifier on coarse fuel (line 39). This line defines the coarse fuel reduction/increase based on the BDA intensity class for BDA type 2. If there are more than two BDA types, the modifiers for each BDA should be input sequentially by BDA.

Harvest section

- Harvest section (line 40). This section begins with a string named "[HARVEST]". The name is specified and upper case is required. This section and all the inputs under this section are required, whether the harvest module is turned on or off. If the harvest module is turned on, the harvest modifier may have effects on fuel loading. Otherwise, this information will be ignored.

- Total harvest events (line 41). This gives the total number of harvest events. This number should be consistent with the number defined in harvest management files.

- Harvest modifier on fine fuel (line 42). This line gives the fine fuel load after harvest event 1. In this example, if the before-harvest fine fuel load was class 0, the after-harvest fine fuel load will increase to class 2.

- Harvest modifier on coarse fuel (line 43). This line gives the coarse fuel load after harvest event 1. In this example, if the before harvest coarse fuel load was class 0, then the after-harvest coarse fuel load will increase to class 3.

- Harvest modifier on fine fuel (line 44). This line gives the fine fuel load after harvest event 2. In this example, if the before-harvest fine fuel load was class 0, then the after-harvest fine fuel load will increase to class 1.

- Harvest modifier on coarse fuel (line 45). This line gives the coarse fuel load after harvest event 2. In this example, if before-harvest coarse fuel load was class 0, then after-harvest coarse fuel load will increase to class 1. If there are more than two harvest events, the modifiers for each harvest event should be input sequentially by harvest event.

15.3 Fuel Rule Input File (fuelRule.dat)

In the fuel rule input file, two tables and some criteria are defined for determining potential fire intensity, potential fire probability, and potential fire risk classes.

15.3.1 Potential fire intensity class

This table lists all the possible combination of fine fuel and coarse fuel classes and defines for each combination the resulting potential fire intensity class. Users can modify this matrix based on their empirical studies.

```
#1   1   1   1   1#      #Fine fuel classes#
#1   2   3   4   5#      #Coarse fuel classes#
 1   1   2   2   3       #Potential fire intensity classes#

#2   2   2   2   2#      #Fine fuel classes#
#1   2   3   4   5#      #Coarse fuel classes#
 1   1   2   3   3       #Potential fire intensity classes#

#3   3   3   3   3#      #Fine fuel classes#
#1   2   3   4   5#      #Coarse fuel classes#
 1   1   2   3   4       #Potential fire intensity classes#

#4   4   4   4   4#      #Fine fuel classes#
#1   2   3   4   5#      #Coarse fuel classes#
 1   2   3   4   5       #Potential fire intensity classes#

#5   5   5   5   5#      #Fine fuel classes#
#1   2   3   4   5#      #Coarse fuel classes#
 2   2   3   4   5       #Potential fire intensity classes#
```

15.3.2 Potential fire probability

This table gives the criteria for classifying potential fire probability (5 classes) from decimal probability data (0.0 ~ 1.0), which is estimated from mean fire return interval and fire history (time since last fire). There are at least two options to generate these probabilities: 1) equal interval, which means the probabilities for the classes are set at equal intervals; and 2) equal area, which means approximately an equal number of active sites (cells) for each class.

The following gives an example of option 1, equal interval. In this example, we calculated the decimal fire probability for all the active cells in the landscape (from mean fire return interval and time since last fire). Then we drew the curve to show in figure 12. Based on the figure, we set the rule as follows:

```
    #Based on equal interval#
0.1  #If decimal fire probability ranges from 0 to 0.1, then it belongs to class 1#
0.2  #If decimal fire probability ranges from 0.1 to 0.2, then it belongs to class 2#
0.3  #If decimal fire probability ranges from 0.2 to 0.3, then it belongs to class 3#
0.4  #If decimal fire probability ranges from 0.3 to 0.4, then it belongs to class 4#
1.0  #If decimal fire probability ranges from 0.4 to 1, then it belongs to class 5#
```

The following provides an example for option 2, equal area. In this example, fire probability for all the cells in the landscape (from mean fire return interval and time since last fire) is calculated using a utility program discussed in section 20.1.4. Based on the calculation, about 1/5 of the total active area has fire probabilities ranging from 0 to 0.08; 1/5 ranging from 0.08 to 0.18; 1/5 from 0.18 to 0.31; 1/5 from 0.31 to 0.51; and 1/5 from 0.51 to 1.0 (fig. 13). Therefore, we set the criteria as:

```
    #Based on equal area#
0.08  #If decimal fire probability ranges from 0 to 0.08, then it belongs to class 1#
0.18  #If decimal fire probability ranges from 0.08 to 0.18, then it belongs to class 2#
0.31  #If decimal fire probability ranges from 0.18 to 0.31, then it belongs to class 3#
0.51  #If decimal fire probability ranges from 0.31 to 0.51, then it belongs to class 4#
1.0   #If decimal fire probability ranges from 0.51 to 1, then it belongs to class 5#
```

15 FUEL MODULE

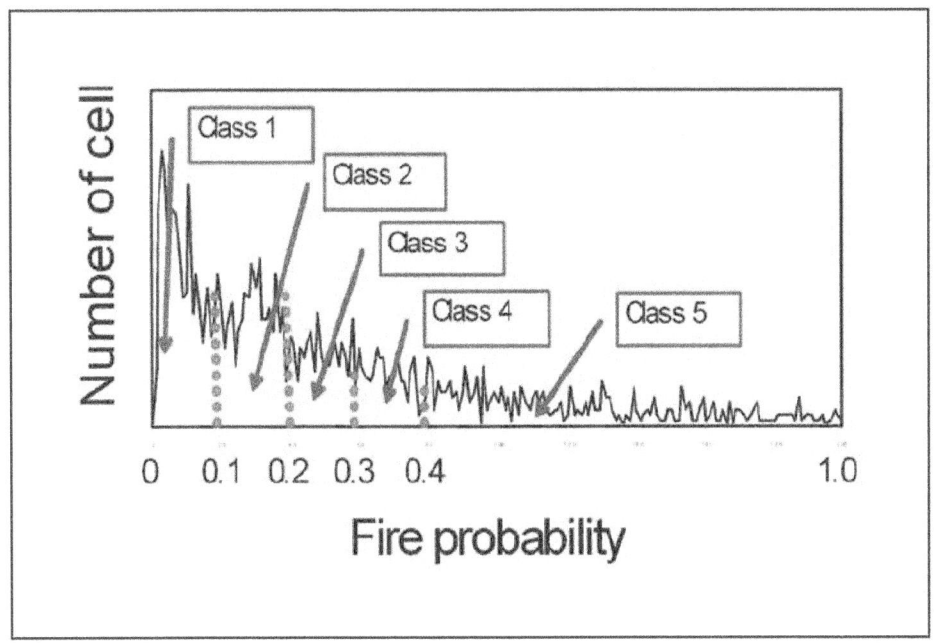

Figure 12. Fire probability classes based on equal interval.

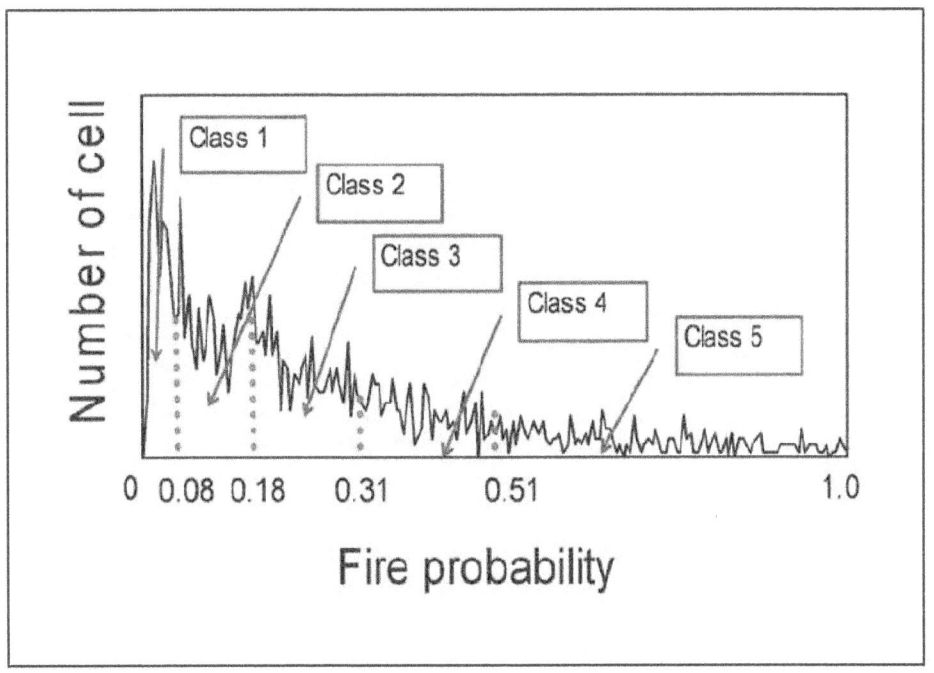

Figure 12. Fire probability classes based on equal area.

15 FUEL MODULE

15.3.3 Potential fire risk

This table lists all the possible combinations of potential fire intensity classes and potential fire probability classes and defines the potential fire risk class for each combination. Users can modifier this table based on their empirical studies. The following is an example in Missouri, which gives high weight to the fine fuel loads.

```
#1   1   1   1   1#      #Potential fire probability class#
#1   2   3   4   5#      #Potential fire intensity class#
 1   1   2   2   3       #Potential fire risk class#

#2   2   2   2   2#      #Potential fire probability class#
#1   2   3   4   5#      #Potential fire intensity class#
 1   1   2   3   3       #Potential fire risk class#

#3   3   3   3   3#      #Potential fire probability class#
#1   2   3   4   5#      #Potential fire intensity class#
 1   1   2   3   4       #Potential fire risk class#

#4   4   4   4   4#      #Potential fire probability class#
#1   2   3   4   5#      #Potential fire intensity class#
 1   2   3   4   5       #Potential fire risk class#

#5   5   5   5   5#      #Potential fire probability class#
#1   2   3   4   5#      #Potential fire intensity class#
 2   2   3   4   5       #Potential fire risk class#
```

15.3.4 Fire regime attributes file (fireRegimeAttr.dat)

Same as section 13.2.

15.3.5 Fuel management event file (fuelMan.dat)

Fuel management event file describes the treatment event. Treatment options include either single or multiple fuel treatment prescriptions. Each prescription is specified by the proportion of cells to be treated, the rotation and frequency of treatment, and the intensity of fine fuel and coarse fuel removal. The treatment events are specified for each management area, and these management boundary maps are defined with a 16-bit Erdas GIS map format. Treatment can be done for fine fuel reduction, coarse fuel reduction, or both fine fuel and coarse fuel reduction. Here we give three examples of different treatment prescriptions. In these examples we have three management areas, and we specify a different fuel treatment prescription for each management area.

15.3.5.1 Example 1—Prescribed burning

Prescribed burning may remove most fine fuels as in the following example:

PRESCRIBEDBURNING						#EVENT LABEL#
1						#management area identifier#
1						#rank algorithm (1=potential fire risk)#
1						#initial decade#
20						#final decade#
2						#reentry interval#
0.10						#proportion of management area for treatment#
2						#minimum potential fire risk for management#
						#Fuel treatment mask#
#0	1	2	3	4	5#	#fine fuel load before management#
0	1	1	1	1	1	#fine fuel load after management#
#0	1	2	3	4	5#	#Coarse fuel load before management#
0	1	2	3	4	5	#Coarse fuel load after management#

- Line 1 is the name of the treatment.
- Line 2 is the identifier of the management area. This number should be consistent with the management boundary map.
- Line 3 is the rank algorithm. At this time there is only one rank algorithm, which is based on potential fire risk.
- Line 4 is the initial decade in which the fuel management will start.
- Line 5 is the final decade in which the fuel management will end.

15.3.5.2 Example 2—Coarse woody debris reduction

Coarse woody debris reduction is used to lower coarse fuels, and the intensity of the removal is defined by the user. For example:

CWDREDUCTION						#EVENT LABEL#
2						#management area identifier#
1						#rank algorithm (1=potential fire risk)#
1						#entry decade#
20						#final decade#
2						#reentry interval#
0.20						#proportion of management area to cut#
2						#minimum potential fire risk for management#
						#Fuel treatment mask#
#0	1	2	3	4	5#	#fine fuel load before management#
1	2	3	4	5	5	#fine fuel load after management#
#0	1	2	3	4	5#	#Coarse fuel load before management#
0	0	0	0	1	2	#Coarse fuel load after management#

The differences of this management prescription with the fine fuels example are:

- Line 2: this management is set for area 2.
- Line 11: this example shows that the high intensity CWD reduction increases fine fuel loads.
- Line 13: here the high intensity CWD reduction results in low coarse fuel loads.

15.3.5.3 Example 3—Prescribed burning + coarse woody debris reduction

Users can define a treatment event that includes both fine fuel and coarse fuel reduction. For example:

```
PRESCRIBEDFIRE+CWDREDUCTION    #EVENT LABEL#
3                              #management area identifier#
1                              #rank algorithm (1=potential fire risk)#
1                              #entry decade#
20                             #final decade#
1                              #reentry interval#
0.15                           #proportion of management area to cut#
2                              #minimum potential fire risk for
                                  management#
                               #Fuel treatment mask#
  #0   1   2   3   4   5#      #fine fuel load before management#
    0   0   0   0   0   1      #fine fuel loads after management#
  #0   1   2   3   4   5#      #Coarse fuel load before management#
    0   0   0   0   1   2      #Coarse fuel load after management#
```

The differences between this management prescription and the others are:

- Line 2: this management is set for area 3.

- Lines 11 and 13: this example shows a high intensity of CWD reduction followed by a high intensity of prescribed burning, resulting in low fine and coarse fuel loads.

16. LANDIS HARVEST MODULE

16.1 Harvest Entry File (harvestInit.dat)

If the harvest entry file (harvestInit.dat) or other file name is set in the LANDIS parameter file, the harvest module will be activated. The following is an example of the harvest entry file.

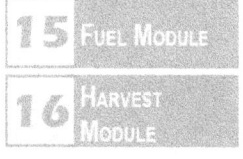

```
0             #1. flag of harvesting, 0-no; 1-on DISABLED#
1             #2. flag of harvesting event, 0-no; 1-on#
0             #3. Stand adjacency flag (0=off, 1=on).  Don't harvest stand
                  if a neighbor was "recently harvested".#
0             #4. n=decade span: Consider an adjacent stand "recently harvested"
                  if it was harvested less than this number of decades ago
0.5           #5. p=proportion:  of cells cut in the last n decades is at least p.#
harvest.dat   #6. Harvest event file#
stand500.gis  #7. Stand identifier input map file#
ma_500.gis    #8. Management area identifier input map file usually rsrvmng8.gis#
stands.log    #9. Harvest stand output file#
ma.log        #10. Harvest management area output file#
```

- Line 1 is old LANDIS (version 2-3.6) timber module switch and this parameter is no longer used.

- Line 2 is the harvest module switch of LANDIS 3.7 and is no longer used.

- Line 3 is stand adjacency switch. If it is turned on, stand adjacency constraints on harvest activity will be enforced. An adjacency constraint prohibits a harvest from occurring on a stand adjacent to another stand that has been recently harvested, in order to prevent very large openings.

- Line 4 defines "recently harvested." If an adjacent stand was harvested less than the number of decades given here, then adjacency constraints must be applied when the stand adjacency switch is turned on.

- Line 5 defines how much of an adjacent stand must have been harvested to trigger the adjacency constraint. For example, if the threshold is 0.5, the adjacency constraint will apply if the proportion of recently harvested cells (defined in line#4) within the stand is larger than this threshold.

- Line 6 is the file name of harvest event file that contains all harvest prescriptions.

- Lines 7 and 8 are file names of stand and management area maps.

- Lines 9 and 10 are file names. These files are used to tabulate harvest history by stand and management area, respectively.

16.2 Harvest Module Input Files

The LANDIS harvest module requires three input files in addition to those already needed by other LANDIS modules: 1) the management area identifier map, 2) the stand identifier map, and 3) the harvest regime input file. Based on the MA identifier map and the stand identifier map each site becomes associated with a single MA and a single stand. The harvest regime input file specifies how harvests will be applied to each MA. These are described in more detail below.

16.2.1 Management area identifier map (ma.gis)

The management area (MA) identifier map indicates which sites are in each MA. MAs are indicated by integers ranging from 1 to the total number of MAs on the map, labeled sequentially. The map value for each site is its corresponding MA. A value of 0 indicates a site that does not belong to any MA and will never be harvested. The format of the MA identifier map is a 16-bit ERDAS GIS file.

16.2.2 Stand identifier map (stand.gis)

The stand identifier map indicates which sites are in each stand. Stands are indicated by integers ranging from 1 to the total number of stands on the map. Note that stand identifiers must be unique over the entire landscape and not just within their designated MA. The map value for each site is its corresponding stand. A value of 0 indicates a site that does not belong to any stand and will never be harvested. The format of the stand identifier map is a 16-bit ERDAS GIS file.

16.2.3 Harvest regime (harvest.dat)

There are six different harvest regimes available for use: 1) one-entry, stand-filling, 2) periodic-entry, stand-filling, 3) two-entry, stand-filling, 4) one-entry, stand-spreading, 5) two-entry, stand-spreading, 6) group selection, 7) periodic-entry-fixed stand, two-entry, stand-filling, and 8) periodic-entry-stand-resampling, two-entry, stand-filling. These regimes can be implemented one or more times in any management area. Singly or in combination these harvest regimes can be used to simulate a wide variety of harvesting practices. Stand-filling harvest regimes are applied to every site in the stand and do not cross stand boundaries. Stand-spreading harvest regimes begin at a focal site in the stand and the harvest terminates when the specified harvest size is reached. If necessary to meet the specified harvest size, stand-spreading harvest regimes will spread into adjacent stands. Stands are prioritized for harvest according to one of four user-specified ranking algorithms that are described in a later section.

16.2.3.1 Harvest mask

The harvest mask specifies by species and age class which cohorts will be removed when a harvest regime is applied, and it specifies which species, if any, will be planted. Planting simply establishes the youngest age cohort of a given species following the harvest of each cell. The format of the harvest mask is similar to the map attribute file in many respects. There is one line for each species, and each line contains a 0 or 1 for each age class. A value of 0 for an age class indicates that the age class should not be harvested for that species. A value of 1 indicates that the age class should be harvested when the regime calls for harvesting on a given site. The first digit in the harvest mask is the planting code. If the planting code is 0 the species is not planted; if the planting code is 1 the species is planted. Harvest regimes and planting codes are further illustrated in later in this section.

16.2.3.2 Stand ranking algorithms

Stands are prioritized for harvest according to one of four user-specified ranking algorithms:

1) Random—stands in a management area are randomly selected for harvest.

2) Stand age—oldest stands in a management area are harvested first. Stand age is computed as the mean of the oldest cohort on each site within the stand.

3) Economic importance—stands are ranked on an index of economic value. Each species is assigned a relative economic value. The value of each age cohort within a species is linearly weighted so that older cohorts are more valuable. The economic value of a site is the sum of the weighted value for each age cohort present, but only includes those age cohorts marked for removal by the harvest mask. The economic value of a stand is the mean of the economic value for each site in the stand. The most valuable stands are harvested first. This ranking algorithm requires additional parameters that indicate the relative economic values of each species and the age of economic maturity for each species.

4) Regulate distribution—stands are ranked by age class so that harvesting over time will result in an even distribution of sites by age classes. This algorithm gives the highest harvest priority to sites and those in age classes found on the greatest number of sites across the management area. The probability of harvest for any given site is calculated by

$$ph = rfs \times e^{ac} \qquad (12)$$

where ph is the probability of harvest for any given site; rfs is relative frequency of sites in the age class; and ac is age class.

5) Flexible regulate distribution—as with regulate distribution, stands can be ranked based on age to produce an even distribution of age classes.

However, this algorithm incorporates a scaling factor that allows the user to control the degree to which stand age influences the probability that a stand will be selected. Low values of the scaling factor result in stands being selected in proportion to their availability on the landscape (thus a scaling factor of 1 behaves similarly to a random rank algorithm), while intermediate values of the scaling factor emulate a regulate distribution, and high values of the scaling factor cause the oldest stands to consistently be selected. The principal advantage of this algorithm is that the user can control the extent to which harvest regulates the distribution of age classes on the landscape and thus the strength of the regulating influence of harvest. Use of this rank algorithm requires the user to provide this scaling factor (as a positive integer) at the end of the list of input variables for a management prescription. When using this algorithm, the probability of harvest for any given site is calculated by

$$ph = rfs \times e^{\frac{ac}{oac}} \times sc \qquad (13)$$

where ph is the probability of harvest for any given site, rfs is relative frequency of sites in the age class and ac is age class, oac is the age of oldest age class in management area, and sc is scaling factor.

16.2.4 Descriptions of harvest regimes (harvest.dat)

16.2.4.1 Harvest regime 1: one-entry, stand-filling

This regime performs one harvest operation on each site in the entire stand during a given decade. This harvest regime can be used to simulate clearcutting, intermediate thinning, single species removal, and removal of trees in specified age classes. Harvested area is specified as a number of sites. A harvest mask (described more fully below) is used to control the removal of age cohorts by species during each one-entry, stand-filling operation.

This regime requires eight arguments:

1) *harvest-regime-id (integer)*. The integer identifying the type of harvest regime.

2) *harvest-regime-label (string, 255 character max)*. A one-word label for the harvest regime. This label is only used to identify entries in the harvest output log files. The label cannot include spaces.

3) *management-area-id (integer)*. The integer identifying the management area where this harvest regime will be implemented. It must be an integer from 1 to the number of management areas.

4) *min-stand-age (integer)*. The minimum age (in years) that a stand must attain to be eligible for harvest.

5) *rank-algorithm (integer)*. The integer identifying the rank algorithm that will be used to determine the order in which stands are harvested. 1 = Random (choose stands randomly), 2 = Stand age (oldest first), 3 = Economic importance (most valuable stands first), 4 = Regulate age class distribution (attempt to produce an even distribution).

6) *entry-decade (integer)*. The decade in which the harvest regime will be implemented. The first iteration in LANDIS is decade 1.

7) *target-cut (integer)*. The total number of sites to harvest over the entire management area. The number of sites harvested may exceed this value because the harvest algorithm will continue to harvest entire stands until the cut target is met or exceeded. This number of sites multiplied by the area of each site (i.e., the area of a cell or pixel) equals the total area to be harvested.

8) *removal-mask*.

Example:

Harvest 100 (*target-cut*) sites from management area 3 (*management-area-id*) in decade 2 (*entry-decade*). Harvest stands in their entirety. Harvest only stands that are at least 70 years (*min-stand-age*) old. Prioritize stands in the management area for harvest using random order (*rank-algorithm*). Remove all age cohorts of every species (i.e., clearcut). No planting.

Coding for harvest regime input file. Note that variables must be entered in the order shown. Comments delimited by # signs are optional. Several harvest regimes can be specified in sequence for a single management area. This example assumes there are four species calibrated in the LANDIS model. The number and order of species in the removal mask must always match that of the LANDIS species attribute file. For clarity in the harvest mask, the planting code is shown in bold-face type followed by the age class harvest codes in normal type.

```
#harvest.dat#
1                          #harvest-regime-id#
SAMPLE-CLEARCUT            #harvest-regime-label#
3                          #management-area-id#
70                         #min-stand-age#
1                          #rank-algorithm#
2                          #entry-decade#
100                        #target-cut#
```

0 111.. repeat for a total of 64 age classes...11	#removal-mask, species 1#
0 111.. repeat for a total of 64 age classes...11	#removal-mask, species 2#
0 111.. repeat for a total of 64 age classes...11	#removal-mask, species 3#
0 111.. repeat for a total of 64 age classes...11	#removal-mask, species 4#

16.2.4.2 Harvest regime 2: periodic-entry, stand-resampling, stand-filling

This regime operates like the one-entry, stand-filling regime except that harvest operations are repeated for a specified number of decades. Harvested area is specified as a proportion of the MA. A harvest mask (described more fully below) is used to control the removal of age cohorts by species during each periodic-entry, stand-filling operation. The algorithm does not necessarily cut the same cells upon each periodic entry.

This regime requires 10 arguments:

1) *harvest-regime-id (integer)*.

2) *harvest-regime-label* (see section 16.2.4.1).

3) *management-area-id (integer)* (see section 16.2.4.1).

4) *min-stand-age (integer)* (see section 16.2.4.1).

5) *rank-algorithm (integer)* (see section 16.2.4.1).

6) *initial-decade (integer)*. The decade in which the harvest regime will start.

7) *final-decade (integer)*. The decade in which the harvest regime will end.

8) *reentry-interval (integer)*. The number of decades between repeated implementation of the harvest action. The harvest action is always implemented in *initial-decade* and it is repeated every *reentry-interval* decades.

9) *target-proportion (real)*. The proportion of sites in the management area to be treated with each harvest action.

10) *removal-mask.*

Example:

Harvest 1/10 (*target-proportion*) of sites from management area 15 (*management-area-id*) every 2 decades (*reentry-interval*) beginning in decade 1 (*initial-decade*) and ending in decade 25 (*final-decade*). Harvest stands in their entirety. Harvest only stands that are at least 50 years (*min-stand-age*) old. Prioritize stands in the management area for harvest using stand age (*rank-algorithm*). Remove age cohorts of every species, but only harvest those cohorts older than 30 years. No planting.

Coding for harvest regime input file. Note that variables must be entered in the order shown. Comments delimited by # signs are optional. Several harvest regimes can be specified in sequence for a single management area. This example assumes there are four species calibrated in the LANDIS model. The number and order of species in the removal mask must always match that of the LANDIS species attribute file. For clarity in the harvest mask, the planting code is shown in bold-face type followed by the age class harvest codes in normal type.

```
2                                              #harvest-regime-id#
SAMPLE-PERIODIC-HARVEST                        #harvest-regime-label#
15                                             #management-area-id#
50                                             #min-stand-age#
2                                              #rank-algorithm#
1                                              #initial-decade#
25                                             #final-decade#
2                                              #reentry-interval#
0.1                                            #target-proportion#
0 000111.. repeat for a total of 64 age classes...11   #removal-mask, species 1#
0 000111.. repeat for a total of 64 age classes...11   #removal-mask, species 2#
0 000111.. repeat for a total of 64 age classes...11   #removal-mask, species 3#
0 000111.. repeat for a total of 64 age classes...11   #removal-mask, species 4#
```

16.2.4.3 Harvest regime 3: two-entry, stand-filling

This regime performs one harvest operation on each site in the entire stand during a given decade. It differs from the one-entry, stand-filling regime in that it keeps track of which sites were harvested. After a specified number of decades the previously harvested sites are revisited and a second harvest operation is applied. This harvest regime can be used to simulate shelterwood and seedtree harvests. Harvested area is specified as a number of sites. A harvest mask (described more fully below) is used to control the removal of age cohorts by species during each of the two harvest activities.

This regime requires 10 arguments:

1) *harvest-regime-id (integer)* (see section 16.2.4.1).

2) *harvest-regime-label* (see section 16.2.4.1).

3) *management-area-id (integer)* (see section 16.2.4.1).

4) *min-stand-age (integer)* (see section 16.2.4.1).

5) *rank-algorithm (integer)* (see section 16.2.4.1).

6) *first-entry-decade* (see section 16.2.4.1).

7) *reentry-decade* (see section 16.2.4.1).

8) *target-cut (integer)* (see section 16.2.4.1).

9) *first-entry-removal-mask (integers: planting code followed by a 0 or 1 for each age class cohort by species).* This removal mask applies only to the first harvest entry. The removal mask has one line for each species in the map attribute file. The first digit in each line is a planting code that is set to 1 if this species is to be planted after harvest, or set to 0 otherwise. (Planting places the species in the 10-year age class.) The remaining digits in each line have a value of 1 (indicating cut) or a value of 0 (indicating leave) for each age cohort for each species in the map attribute file.

10) *reentry-removal-mask (integers: planting code followed by a 0 or 1 for each age class cohort by species).* This removal mask applies only to the second (final) harvest entry. The removal mask has one line for each species in the map attribute file. The first digit in each line is a planting code that is set to 1 if this species is to be planted after harvest, or set to 0 otherwise. (Planting places the species in the 10-year age class.) The remaining digits in each line have a value of 1 (indicating cut) or a value of 0 (indicating leave) for each age cohort for each species in the map attribute file. See definition above and example below.

Example:

Harvest 2,500 (*target-cut*) sites from management area 43 (*management-area-id*). Perform a shelterwood harvest with the initial harvest in decade 5 (*first-entry-decade*) and the reentry in decade 7 (*reentry-decade*). In the initial harvest retain only cohorts of species 2 and species 4 that are at least 70 years old. In the reentry, harvest the residual overstory (i.e., cohorts of species 2 and 4 that are at least 70 years old). Harvest only stands that are at least 80 years (*min-stand-age*) old. Prioritize stands in the management area for harvest using stand age (*rank-algorithm*). No planting.

Coding for harvest regime input file. Note that variables must be entered in the order shown. Comments delimited by # signs are optional. Several harvest regimes can be specified in sequence for a single management area. This example assumes there are four species calibrated in the LANDIS model. The number and order of species in the removal mask must always match that of the LANDIS species attribute file. For clarity in the harvest mask, the planting code is shown in bold-face type followed by the age class harvest codes in normal type.

3	#harvest-regime-id#
SAMPLE-SHELTERWOOD	#harvest-regime-label#
43	#management-area-id#
80	#min-stand-age#
2	#rank-algorithm#
5	#first-entry-decade#
7	#reentry-decade#
2500	#target-cut#

0 11111111.. repeat for 64 age classes...11	#first-entry-removal-mask, species 1#
0 11111100...repeat for 64 age classes...00	#first-entry-removal-mask, species 2#
0 11111111.. repeat for 64 age classes...11	#first-entry-removal-mask, species 3#
0 11111100...repeat for 64 age classes...00	#first-entry-removal-mask, species 4#

0 00000000...repeat for 64 age classes...00	#reentry-removal-mask, species 1#
0 00000011.. repeat for 64 age classes...11	#reentry-removal-mask, species 2#
0 00000000...repeat for 64 age classes...00	#reentry-removal-mask, species 3#
0 00000011.. repeat for 64 age classes...11	#reentry-removal-mask, species 4#

16.2.4.4 Harvest regime 4: one-entry, stand-spreading

This regime performs like the one-entry, stand-filling regime except that harvests can spread beyond stand boundaries. The total harvested area for a given decade is specified as a number of sites. The size of individual harvest events is drawn from a normal distribution with mean and standard deviation specified by the user. Each harvest event starts at a random site on the stand. It expands until the specified target size is reached. If necessary to meet the specified harvest size, the harvest will spread into adjacent stands, but each stand is completely harvested before adjacent stands are harvested. This harvest regime can be used to simulate clearcutting, intermediate thinning, single-species removal, and removal of trees in specified age classes. A harvest mask (described more fully below) is used to control the removal of age cohorts by species during each harvest operation.

This regime requires 10 arguments:

1) *harvest-regime-id (integer).*

2) *harvest-regime-label* (see section 16.2.4.1).

3) *management-area-id (integer)* (see section 16.2.4.1).

4) *min-stand-age (integer)* (see section 16.2.4.1).

5) *rank-algorithm (integer)* (see section 16.2.4.1).

6) *entry-decade (integer)* (see section 16.2.4.1).

7) *target-cut* (see section 16.2.4.1).

8) *mean-harvest-size.* Mean number of sites included in each harvest. Mean must be ≥ 1. The size of each harvest event is drawn from a normal distribution with this mean and a specified standard deviation (see below).

9) *standard-deviation.* Standard deviation (expressed as number of sites) of the distribution used to specify harvest size. The range of harvest sizes will generally not exceed the mean size ± 3 standard deviations.

10) *removal-mask (integers: planting code followed by a 0 or 1 for each age class cohort by species).* The removal mask has one line for each species in the map attribute file. The first digit in each line is a planting code that is set to 1 if this species is to be planted after harvest, or set to 0 otherwise.

(Planting places the species in the 10-year age class.) The remaining digits in each line have a value of 1 (indicating cut) or a value of 0 (indicating leave) for each age cohort for each species in the map attribute file. See definition above and example below.

Example:

Harvest 5,000 (*target-cut*) sites from management area 6 (*management-area-id*) in decade 3 (*entry-decade*). Harvests should have a mean size of 100 sites and a standard deviation of 20. Initiate harvests only in stands that are at least 60 years (*min-stand-age*) old. Prioritize stands in the management area for harvest using random order (*rank-algorithm*). Remove only age cohorts that are at least 20 years old. Plant species 2 and species 3 following harvest.

Coding for harvest regime input file. Note that variables must be entered in the order shown. Comments delimited by # signs are optional. Several harvest regimes can be specified in sequence for a single management area. This example assumes there are four species calibrated in the LANDIS model. The number and order of species in the removal mask must always match that of the LANDIS species attribute file. For clarity in the harvest mask, the planting code is shown in bold-face type followed by the age class harvest codes in normal type.

```
4                    #harvest-regime-id#
LARGE-OPENINGS       #harvest-regime-label#
6                    #management-area-id#
60                   #min-stand-age#
1                    #rank-algorithm#
3                    #entry-decade#
5000                 #target-cut#
100                  #mean-harvest-size#
20                   #standard-deviation#
```

```
0 011...repeat for a total of 64 age classes...11    #removal-mask, species 1#
1 011...repeat for a total of 64 age classes...11    #removal-mask, species 2#
1 011...repeat for a total of 64 age classes...11    #removal-mask, species 3#
0 011...repeat for a total of 64 age classes...11    #removal-mask, species 4#
```

16.2.4.5 Harvest regime 5: two-entry, stand-spreading

This regime performs like the two-entry, stand-filling regime except that harvests can spread beyond stand boundaries as they do in the one-entry, stand-spreading regime. The total harvested area for a given decade is specified as a number of sites. The size of individual harvest events is drawn from a normal distribution with mean and standard deviation specified by the user. Each harvest event starts at a random site on the stand. It expands until the specified target size is reached. If necessary to meet the specified harvest size, the harvest will spread into adjacent stands, but each stand is completely harvested before adjacent stands are harvested. After a specified number of decades the previously harvested sites are revisited and a second harvest operation is applied. This harvest regime can be used to simulate shelterwood and seedtree harvests. A harvest mask (described more fully below) is used to control the removal of age cohorts by species during each of the two activities.

This regime requires 12 arguments:

1) *harvest-regime-id.*

2) *harvest-regime-label* (see section 16.2.4.1).

3) *management-area-id (integer)* (see section 16.2.4.1).

4) *min-stand-age (integer)* (see section 16.2.4.1).

5) *rank-algorithm (integer)* (see section 16.2.4.1).

6) *first-entry-decade* (see section 16.2.4.1).

7) *reentry-decade* (see section 16.2.4.1).

8) *target-cut* (see section 16.2.4.1).

9) *mean-harvest-size.* Mean number of sites included in each harvest. Mean must be ≥ 1. The size of each harvest event is drawn from a normal distribution with this mean and a specified standard deviation (see below).

10) *standard-deviation.* Standard deviation (expressed as number of sites) of the distribution used to specify harvest size. The range of harvest sizes will generally not exceed the mean size ± 3 standard deviations.

11) *first-entry-removal-mask (integers: planting code followed by a 0 or 1 for each age class cohort by species).* This removal mask applies only to the first harvest entry. The removal mask has one line for each species in the map attribute file. The first digit in each line is a planting code that is set to 1 if this species is to be planted after harvest, or set to 0 otherwise. (Planting places the species in the 10-year age class.) The remaining digits in each line have a value of 1 (indicating cut) or a value of 0 (indicating leave) for each age cohort for each species in the map attribute file. See definition above and example below.

12) *reentry-removal-mask (integers: planting code followed by a 0 or 1 for each age class cohort by species).* This removal mask applies only to the second (final) harvest entry. The removal mask has one line for each species in the map attribute file. The first digit in each line is a planting code that is set to 1 if this species is to be planted after harvest, or set to 0 otherwise. (Planting places the species in the 10-year age class.) The remaining digits in each line have a value of 1 (indicating cut) or a value of 0 (indicating leave) for each age cohort for each species in the map attribute file. See definition above and example below.

16 HARVEST MODULE

Example:

Harvest 7,000 (*target-cut*) sites from management area 19 (*management-area-id*). Perform a shelterwood harvest with the initial harvest in decade 1 (*first-entry-decade*) and the reentry in decade 2 (*reentry-decade*). Harvests should have a mean size of 30 sites and a standard deviation of 5. Initiate harvests only in stands that are at least 40 years (*min-stand-age*) old. In the initial harvest retain only cohorts of species 2 and species 4 that are at least 60 years old. In the reentry, harvest the residual overstory (i.e., cohorts of species 2 and 4 that are at least 60 years old). Prioritize stands in the management area for harvest using stand age (*rank-algorithm*). No planting.

Coding for harvest regime input file. Note that variables must be entered in the order shown. Comments delimited by # signs are optional. Several harvest regimes can be specified in sequence for a single management area. This example assumes there are four species calibrated in the LANDIS model. The number and order of species in the removal mask must always match that of the LANDIS species attribute file. For clarity in the harvest mask, the planting code is shown in bold-face type followed by the age class harvest codes in normal type.

5	#harvest-regime-id#
SAMPLE-SHELTERWOOD	#harvest-regime-label#
19	#management-area-id#
40	#min-stand-age#
2	#rank-algorithm#
1	#first-entry-decade#
2	#reentry-decade#
7000	#target-cut#
30	#mean-harvest-size#
5	#standard-deviation#

0 11111111.. repeat for 64 age classes...11	#first-entry-removal-mask, species 1#
0 11111000.. repeat for 64 age classes...00	#first-entry-removal-mask, species 2#
0 11111111.. repeat for 64 age classes...11	#first-entry-removal-mask, species 3#
0 11111000.. repeat for 64 age classes...00	#first-entry-removal-mask, species 4#

0 00000000...repeat for 64 age classes...00	#reentry-removal-mask, species 1#
0 00000111...repeat for 64 age classes...11	#reentry-removal-mask, species 2#
0 00000000...repeat for 64 age classes...00	#reentry-removal-mask, species 3#
0 00000111...repeat for 64 age classes...11	#reentry-removal-mask, species 4#

16.2.4.6 Harvest regime 6: group selection

As the name implies, this management regime is used to simulate group selection harvest. The area to be treated with a group selection harvest is specified as a proportion of the stands in the management area. Once a stand is selected for group selection no other harvest regime will treat that stand. Group selection harvests begin at a specified decade and are reapplied to the same stands at a specified interval. The user specifies the proportion of sites in each stand to be removed at each entry. Group size is drawn from a normal distribution with mean and standard deviation specified by the user. Group placement is random but constrained so that groups do not touch one another. Once harvested, sites cannot be re-harvested until the number of elapsed years is equal to the reentry interval divided by the proportion of sites to be harvested in each entry.

This regime requires 12 arguments:

1) *harvest-regime-id.*

2) *harvest-regime-label* (see section 16.2.4.1).

3) *management-area-id* (see section 16.2.4.1).

4) *min-stand-age* (see section 16.2.4.1).

5) *rank-algorithm (integer)* (see section 16.2.4.1).

6) *initial-decade (integer)* (see section 16.2.4.1).

7) *reentry-interval (integer)* (see section 16.2.4.1).

8) *target-proportion (real)* (see section 16.2.4.1).

9) *stand-proportion-denominator (integer).* The denominator of the fractional portion of the stand that is to be harvested (i.e., placed into group openings) during each entry. For example, to harvest 1/5 of the stand in each entry, set the value of stand-proportion-denominator to 5.

10) *mean-group-size (real)*. The mean size of group openings expressed as a number of sites. Mean must be ≥ 1.

11) *standard-deviation (real)*. The standard deviation of group opening size expressed as a number of sites.

12) *removal-mask (integers: planting code followed by a 0 or 1 for each age class cohort by species)*. The removal mask has one line for each species in the map attribute file. The first digit in each line is a planting code that is set to 1 if this species is to be planted after harvest, or set to 0 otherwise. (Planting places the species in the 10-year age class). The remaining digits in each line have a value of 1 (indicating cut) or a value of 0 (indicating leave) for each age cohort for each species in the map attribute file. See definition above and example below.

Example:

Perform a repeated series of group selection harvests on 75 percent (*target-proportion*) of the stands in management area 19 (*management-area-id*). Begin group selection harvest in decade 1 (*first-entry-decade*) and repeat each decade (*reentry-interval*) for the duration of the simulation. The stands selected for group selection harvesting will not be harvested by any other regime for the duration of the simulation. Prioritize stands in the management area for harvest using stand age (*rank-algorithm*). At each entry the area in group openings in each stand should equal 1/12 (1/*stand-proportion-denominator*) of the total stand area. Group selection openings should have a mean size of 3 sites and a standard deviation of 1. Initiate harvests only in stands that are at least 40 years (*min-stand-age*) old. Harvest all species in all age classes. Plant species 1 after harvest.

Coding for harvest regime input file. Note that variables must be entered in the order shown. Comments delimited by # signs are optional. Several harvest regimes can be specified in sequence for a single management area. This example assumes there are four species calibrated in the LANDIS model. The number and order of species in the removal mask must always match that of the LANDIS species attribute file. For clarity in the harvest mask, the planting code is shown in boldface type followed by the age class harvest codes in normal type.

```
6                         #harvest-regime-id#
SAMPLE-GROUP-SELECTION     #harvest-regime-label#
19                        #management-area-id#
40                        #min-stand-age#
2                         #rank-algorithm#
1                         #initial-decade#
1                         #reentry-interval#
0.75                      #target-proportion#
12                        #stand-proportion-denominator
3                         #mean-group-size#
1                         #standard-deviation#
```

```
1 111.. repeat for a total of 64 age classes...11    #removal-mask, species 1#
0 111.. repeat for a total of 64 age classes...11    #removal-mask, species 2#
0 111.. repeat for a total of 64 age classes...11    #removal-mask, species 3#
0 111.. repeat for a total of 64 age classes...11    #removal-mask, species 4#
```

16 HARVEST MODULE

16.2.4.7 Harvest regime 7: periodic-entry-fixed-stand, two-entry, stand-filling

This regime closely resembles harvest regime 3 (two-entry, stand-filling). It performs one harvest operation on each site in stands during a given decade. It keeps track of which sites were harvested and after a specified number of decades the previously harvested sites are revisited and a second harvest operation (with its own harvest mask) is applied. It differs from regime 3 in that this pair of harvest entries is repeated periodically throughout the course of the simulation. Note this pair of entries is always applied to the same stands that were selected based upon the ranking algorithm during the first-entry-decade. This periodic design allows users to repeated a pair of entries many times over the coarse of a long simulation. Thus, the need for users to rewrite similar harvest regimes multiple times in the harvest.dat file is reduced and two entry regimes like shelterwood and seed tree harvests can be simulated conveniently in long runs. The harvested area is specified as a number of sites. A pair of harvest masks (described more fully below) is used to control the removal of age cohorts by species during each of the two harvest activities. Note this pair of entries is always applied to the same stands that were selected based upon the ranking algorithm during the first-entry-decade (fixed stand).

This regime requires 11 arguments:

1) *harvest-regime-id (integer)* (set this value to 7 to select this regime).

2) *harvest-regime-label* (see section 16.2.4.1).

3) *management-area-id (integer)* (see section 16.2.4.1).

4) *min-stand-age (integer in years not decades)* (see section 16.2.4.1).

5) *rank-algorithm (integer)* (see section 16.2.4.1).

6) *first-entry-decade* (see section 16.2.4.1).

7) *decades until second entry.* This value is the number of decades that will elapse between the first entry and second entry for each application of this regime to a stand.

8) *return interval.* This is the number of decades after the first-entry when the two entries will be applied to the exact same stands. Note this pair of entries will continue to repeat at this interval throughout the course of the simulation.

9) *target-cut (integer)* (see section 16.2.4.1).

10) *first-entry-removal-mask.* This removal mask applies to the first harvest entry for each pair of entries that are applied to the selected stands throughout the course of the simulation. The removal mask has one line for each species in the map attribute file. The digits in each line have a value of 1 (indicating cut) or a value of 0 (indicating leave) for each age cohort for each species in the map attribute file.

11) *reentry-removal-mask.* This removal mask applies to the second harvest entry for each pair of entries that are applied to the selected stands throughout the course of the simulation. The removal mask has one line for each species in the map attribute file. The digits in each line have a value of 1 (indicating cut) or a value of 0 (indicating leave) for each age cohort for each species in the map attribute file. See definition above and example below.

Example:

Harvest 5,753 (target-cut) sites from management area 15 (management-area-id). During decade 1 (first-entry-decade) stands will be selected based upon the stand age rank algorithm and set aside for the duration of the simulation. Only stands that are at least 40 years (min-stand-age) old will be selected for harvest. These stands will be cut according to the initial harvest mask of a shelterwood prescription. These same stands will be revisited in decade 3 (first-entry + decades until second entry) and cut according to the reentry mask of a shelterwood prescription. Initial harvests for this shelterwood prescription will retain only cohorts of species 2 and species 4 that are at least 70 years old. In the reentry harvest for this shelterwood prescription, residual overstory (i.e., cohorts of species 2 and 4 that are at least 70 years old) will be harvested. This same pair of harvests will be repeated in these same stands during decade 90 (first-entry + return interval) and at other 8-decade increments for the duration of the simulation (e.g., decade 170, 250, etc.).

Coding for harvest regime input file. Note that variables must be entered in the order shown. Comments delimited by # signs are optional. Several harvest regimes can be specified in sequence for a single management area. This example assumes that there are four species calibrated in the LANDIS model. The number and order of species in the removal mask must always match that of the LANDIS species attribute file.

7	#harvest-regime-id#
Periodic-fixed-Shelterwood	#harvest-regime-label#
15	#management area identifier#
40	#minimum stand age (in years)#
2	#rank algorithm#
1	#entry decade#
2	#decades until second entry#
8	#return interval#
5753	#target number of sites to cut#

0 11111111.. repeat for 64 age classes...11	#first-entry-removal-mask, species 1#
0 11111100...repeat for 64 age classes...00	#first-entry-removal-mask, species 2#
0 11111111.. repeat for 64 age classes...11	#first-entry-removal-mask, species 3#
0 11111100...repeat for 64 age classes...00	#first-entry-removal-mask, species 4#
0 00000000...repeat for 64 age classes...00	#reentry-removal-mask, species 1#
0 00000011.. repeat for 64 age classes...11	#reentry-removal-mask, species 2#
0 00000000...repeat for 64 age classes...00	#reentry-removal-mask, species 3#
0 00000011.. repeat for 64 age classes...11	#reentry-removal-mask, species 4#

16 HARVEST MODULE

16.2.4.8 Harvest regime 8: periodic-entry-stand-resampling, two-entry, stand-filling

This regime closely resembles harvest regime 7 (periodic-entry-fixed-stand, two-entry, stand-filling) and is valuable for many of the same reasons. It supplies a convenient way to repeat two-entry, stand-filling harvests throughout the course of a simulation without having to write multiple harvest regimes. The principal difference is that during each period when this regime revisits a management area to implement an initial harvest it selects a new stand based upon the designated stand ranking algorithm and the current conditions on the landscape. In contrast, regime 7 selected stands during the initial entry decade and revisited these same stands during all second entries and periods of reentry for the duration of the simulation. Thus, stands that are selected by regime 8 are only set aside as unavailable to other harvest regimes during the period between an initial entry and a second entry. This makes regime 8 a more convenient regime to use if you want to initiate new two-entry harvests during each decade of the simulation and are not worried about locking particular stands into management by a single regime for the duration of the simulation. As with regime 7, the harvested area is specified as a number of sites, and 2 harvest masks (described more fully below) are used to control the removal of age cohorts by species during each of the two entries into a particular stand.

This regime requires 11 arguments:

1) *harvest-regime-id (integer)* (set this value to 8 to select this regime).

2) *harvest-regime-label* (see section 16.2.4.1).

3) *management-area-id (integer)* (see section 16.2.4.1).

4) *min-stand-age (integer in years not decades)* (see section 16.2.4.1).

5) *rank-algorithm (integer)* (see section 16.2.4.1).

6) *first-entry-decade* (see section 16.2.4.1).

7) *decades-until-second-entry.* This value is the number of decades that will elapse between the first entry and second entry for each application of this regime to a stand.

8) *return interval.* This number of decades after the first entry when the two entries will be applied to the exact same stands. Note this pair of entries will continue to repeat at this interval throughout the course of the simulation.

9) *target-cut (integer)* (see section 16.2.4.1).

10) *first-entry-removal-mask.* This removal mask applies to the first harvest entry for each pair of entries that are applied to the selected stands throughout the course of the simulation. The removal mask has one line for each species in the map attribute file. The digits in each line have a value of 1 (indicating cut) or a value of 0 (indicating leave) for each age cohort for each species in the map attribute file.

11) *reentry-removal-mask.* This removal mask applies to the second harvest entry for each pair of entries that are applied to the selected stands throughout the course of the simulation. The removal mask has one line for each species in the map attribute file. The digits in each line have a value of 1 (indicating cut) or a value of 0 (indicating leave) for each age cohort for each species in the map attribute file. See definition above and example below.

Example:

Select 1,513 (*target-cut*) sites from management area 1 (*management-area-id*) during each decade of the simulation (*reentry interval*) for use in a shelterwood harvest. Only stands that are at least 30 years (*min-stand-age*) old will be selected for harvest. During decade 1 (*first-entry decade*), begin this regime by selecting stands according to the stand age rank algorithm and cutting them according to the initial harvest mask of a shelterwood prescription. These same stands will be revisited in decade 4 (*first-entry + decades-until-second-entry*) and cut according to the reentry mask of a shelterwood prescription. Apply this regime to management area 1 during each decade (*return interval*) for the duration of the simulation. Note new stands will be selected based upon the stand age rank algorithm during each reapplication of this prescription and selected stands are only unavailable to other regimes during the interval between the initial harvest and the reentry harvest. Initial harvests for this shelterwood prescription will retain only cohorts of species 2 and species 4 that are at least 70 years old. In the reentry harvest for this shelterwood prescription, residual overstory (i.e., cohorts of species 2 and 4 that are at least 70 years old) will be harvested.

Coding for harvest regime input file. Note that variables must be entered in the order shown. Comments delimited by # signs are optional. Several harvest regimes can be specified in sequence for a single management area. This example assumes there are four species calibrated in the LANDIS model. The number and order of species in the removal mask must always match that of the LANDIS species attribute file.

```
8                                       #harvest-regime-id#
Periodic-Resampling-Shelterwood         #harvest-regime-label#
1                                       #management area identifier#
30                                      #minimum stand age (in years)#
2                                       #rank algorithm#
1                                       #entry decade#
3                                       #decades until second entry#
1                                       #return interval#
1513                                    #target number of sites to cut#
```

```
0 11111111.. repeat for 64 age classes...11   #first-entry-removal-mask, species 1#
0 11111100...repeat for 64 age classes...00   #first-entry-removal-mask, species 2#
0 11111111.. repeat for 64 age classes...11   #first-entry-removal-mask, species 3#
0 11111100...repeat for 64 age classes...00   #first-entry-removal-mask, species 4#
0 00000000...repeat for 64 age classes...00   #reentry-removal-mask, species 1#
0 00000011.. repeat for 64 age classes...11   #reentry-removal-mask, species 2#
0 00000000...repeat for 64 age classes...00   #reentry-removal-mask, species 3#
0 00000011.. repeat for 64 age classes...11   #reentry-removal-mask, species4#
```

17. OUTPUT FILES

17.1 GIS Map Files

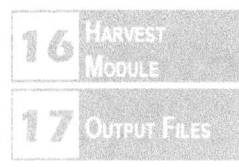

The majority of LANDIS output is as ERDAS GIS files. These files are in 8-bit format and have accompanying trailer (.TRL) files. The trailer files are not complete; they do not contain output statistics.

For each iteration a GIS file (and its accompanying trailer file) will be created for each output reclassification method. A GIS file showing the ages of the oldest cohort on each cell is also created. Additional files will be created for fire, wind, BDA, fuel, and harvest modules if they are turned on before the model run. The names of the files will be AGE, FIRE, WIND, HARVEST (in each module parameter file discussed in the previous chapters), or the appropriate output reclassification method name followed by the year number.

Three other GIS files are also created and placed in the output directory. The first is a map of the land types named LU.GIS (same as land type map input file landtype.gis). The second is a final map of fires. It shows all fires that occurred throughout time. The third is the final map of wind disturbances. In the case of an overlap the most recent fire or wind is displayed. The names of the files are given in the disturbance file.

17.1.1 Species GIS file

The pixel values within species GIS files are described by the corresponding RCS file. Pixel value 0 always denotes area outside the simulation boundaries; 1 denotes water; and 2 denotes lowland and other nonactive simulated areas. Pixel value 3 will correspond to the first type defined in the RCS file, 4, the second, and so on. Pixel value 255, the highest value, always denotes "other."

17.1.2 Species age GIS file

The first three pixel values (0-2) within species age GIS files are defined exactly as they are for the species GIS file. Pixel value 3 denotes species age from 0-10, 4 denotes 10-20, 5 denotes 20-30, and so forth. Pixel value 255 denotes "other."

17.1.3 Age group GIS file

The first three pixel values (0-2) within species age GIS files are defined exactly as they are for the species GIS file. Pixel value 3 denotes the oldest species age 0-30, 4 denotes 30-60, 5 denotes 60-90, and so forth. Pixel value of 255 denotes "other."

17.1.4 Disturbance GIS file

The first three pixel values (0-2) within disturbance GIS files are defined exactly as they are for the species GIS file. Pixel values 3-7 represent fire or wind intensity classes 1-5, respectively. For BDA disturbance GIS files, pixel values 3-5 represent BDA intensity classes 1-3, respectively.

17.1.5 Harvest GIS file

There are two types of harvest output GIS files, harvest types and harvest history. Harvest type maps record IDs of the last harvest regime applied on each pixel. Harvest history maps record the year since last harvest for each pixel.

17.2 Trailer File

Each output GIS file has an associated ERDAS 7.4 trailer file that contains the map legend.

17.3 Log Files

The files WIND.LOG and FIRE.LOG contain a spreadsheet-compatible log of the fire and wind events that occurred during the simulation. Each wind log file entry records the year when the disturbance occurred, the map coordinates where the wind started, disturbance size, damage size, and number of cohorts killed. Disturbance size is the number of cells that were checked for a given disturbance, whereas damage size is the number of cells in which at least one age cohort was removed due to the disturbance.

The fire log file records additional disturbance information for each land type.

The files MA.LOG and STAND.LOG contain spreadsheet-compatible logs of harvest summarized by management area and stand, respectively.

The file FUEL.LOG contains a spreadsheet-compatible log of the fine fuel load, coarse fuel load, potential fire probability, potential fire intensity, and potential fire risk for each simulation year. The output follows this order: simulation year, number of cells in each fine fuel load class (0 to 5), average fine fuel load, number of cells in each coarse fuel load class (0 to 5), average coarse fuel load, number of cells in each potential fire probability class (0 to 5), average potential fire probability, number of cells in each potential fire intensity class (0 to 5), average potential fire intensity, number of cells in each potential fire risk class (0 to 5), and average potential fire risk.

18. RUNNING THE PROGRAM

18.1 Using LANDIS Input Interface

18.1.1 LI.exe

LANDIS Interface (LI) is an integrated tool that can be used to edit LANDIS input parameter files, to run the LANDIS system, and to view the LANDIS output maps in an integrated environment. LANDIS Interface is an MFC MDI application developed with Visual C++ 6.0.

The parameter files used by the LANDIS system are composed of a main configuration file, several first-level configuration files linked to the main configuration file, and several second-level configuration files linked to the first-level configuration files. The LANDIS system accepts a main configuration file as a command line parameter that passes the information and setting into the program, and each module of the LANDIS system uses the first-level and the second-level configuration files to retrieve more information.

LANDIS Interface program can automatically open the main configuration file and the corresponding first-level configuration files for editing. In addition, the program can open any configuration file specified by users manually. The program can also call LANDIS Viewer to display the *.gis map files that are used as part of the input of LANDIS system.

Once a main configuration file is opened, the program can cause the LANDIS system to run by using this main configuration file as the input parameter. After that, the program can call LANDIS Viewer to display the output results (fig. 14).

18.1.2 Menu

The menu of the LANDIS Interface is divided into the following sub-menus:

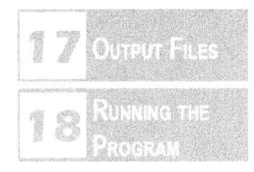

1. File Menu
    a. New
    Create a new document (application project). The content of this document is automatically set by the template.

    b. Open
    Open an existing main configuration file.

    c. Close
    Close the active document.

    d. Save
    Save the active document.

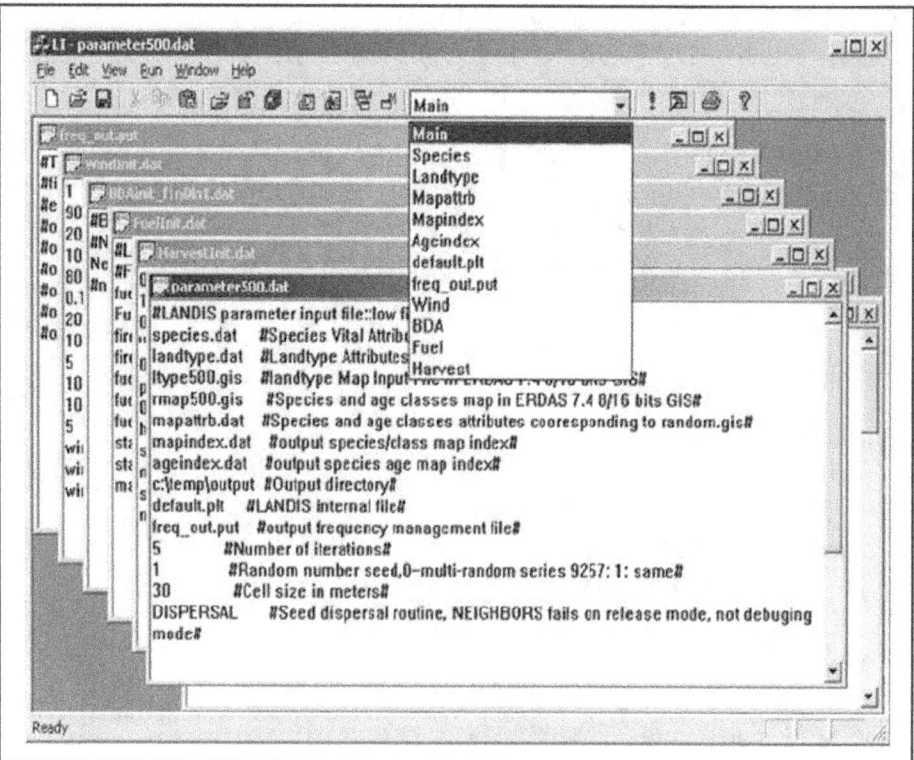

Figure 14. The main user interface of LANDIS. The interface is a typical MFC MDI program composed of menu bar, tool bar, edit windows, and status bar.

e. Save as
   Save the active document with a new name.

f. Open related configuration file
   Open any configuration file except the main configuration file. (If a file name is selected in the document, the file will be opened; otherwise, a dialog is shown to let user select the file name.)

g. Open *.gis map file
   Open an existing *.gis map file and call LANDIS Viewer to display this file. (If a file name is selected in the document, the file will be opened; otherwise, a dialog is shown to let user select the file name.)

h. Print
   Print the active document.

i. Print Preview
   Preview the pages before printing.

j. Print Setup
   Change the printer and printing options.

k. Most Recent Files List
   Show the most recently opened file list, and allow opening of these files directly.

l. Exit
   Exit the LANDIS Interface.

18 RUNNING THE PROGRAM

2. Edit Menu

    a. Undo
       Undo the last action.

    b. Cut
       Cut the selection and put it on clipboard.

    c. Copy
       Copy the selection and put it on clipboard.

    d. Paste
       Insert the clipboard contents.

3. View Menu

    a. Toolbar
       Show or hide the Toolbar.

    b. Status Bar
       Show or hide the Status Bar.

4. Run Menu

    a. Open All Config Files
       Open all the first-level configuration files related to the main
       configuration file.

    b. Save All Config Files
       Save all the first-level configuration files related to the main
       configuration file.

    c. Close All Config Files
       Close all the first-level configuration files related to the main
       configuration file.

    d. Launch LANDIS System
       Call the LANDIS system and use the main configuration file as the
       input parameter.

    e. Launch LANDIS Viewer
       Call LANDIS Viewer to display the running results of the LANDIS
       system.

    f. Options
       Change the options, including the file location of the LANDIS system
       and LANDIS Viewer, and the default color palette for LANDIS
       Viewer.

18 RUNNING THE PROGRAM

5. Window Menu

    a. Main Configuration File
       Jump to the Main Configuration File.

    b. Windows list
       Show the windows list and jump to the selected window.

6. Help Menu

    a. About
       Display the program information, version, and copyright.

18.1.3 Toolbar

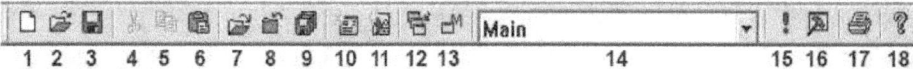

The toolbar is shown in the upper part of the window. Each button works exactly the same as its corresponding menu item. The corresponding menu item for each button (from left to right) is:

1.   File > New
2.   File > Open
3.   File > Save
4.   Edit > Cut
5.   Edit > Copy
6.   Edit > Paste
7.   Run > Open All Config Files
8.   Run > Close All Config Files
9.   Run > Save All Config Files
10. File > Open related configuration file
11. File > Open *.gis map file
12. Window > Windows List
13. Window > Main Configuration File
14. Windows List for the first-level configuration files. It can be used to rapidly jump to the main configuration file or a first-level configuration file.
15. Run > Launch LANDIS System
16. Run > Launch LANDIS Viewer
17. File > Print
18. Help > About

18.2 Through Windows DOS Prompt

At a Windows Command prompt, go to the directory that contains your LANDIS input file, then type LANDIS followed by the parameter file name. If you do not specify a parameter file then LANDIS will show the correct syntax and terminate:

>   Usage: LANDIS [-argument [...]] <input file>

arguments:

>   -e: the years environmental change interpreted (page 5.9)

>   -h: this help menu

>   -p: input file help

[ ] indicates that the argument is optional. < > indicates the argument is required. For more information about LANDIS input files, refer to chapters 8-13.

19. LANDIS OUTPUT VIEWER (LV.EXE)

19.1 Overview

LANDIS Viewer is a tool to view 8-bit/16-bit GIS maps or LANDIS output maps. The viewer is a dialog-based windows application developed using Visual C++ 6.0. It loads one GIS map file or a whole LANDIS output directory and displays those maps using a user-specified color palette. When it loads a whole LANDIS output directory, LANDIS Viewer arranges those LANDIS outputs by species/disturbances and time sequences and provides an efficient way to choose species/disturbances and to navigate between time sequences.

19.2 Main User Interface

The main user interface of LANDIS Viewer is shown in figure 15.

The main user interface of LANDIS Viewer is composed of six components: title bar, time sequence navigation controls, color palette selection control, species list, map display, and legend list.

The title bar is used to show status information for the currently displayed map including file path, species name, and the number of years in time sequence. It also shows error messages if errors occur.

The title bar is used to show status information for the currently displayed map including its file path, species name, and year index. It also shows error messages if errors occur.

Time sequence navigation controls are used to navigate in the time sequences.

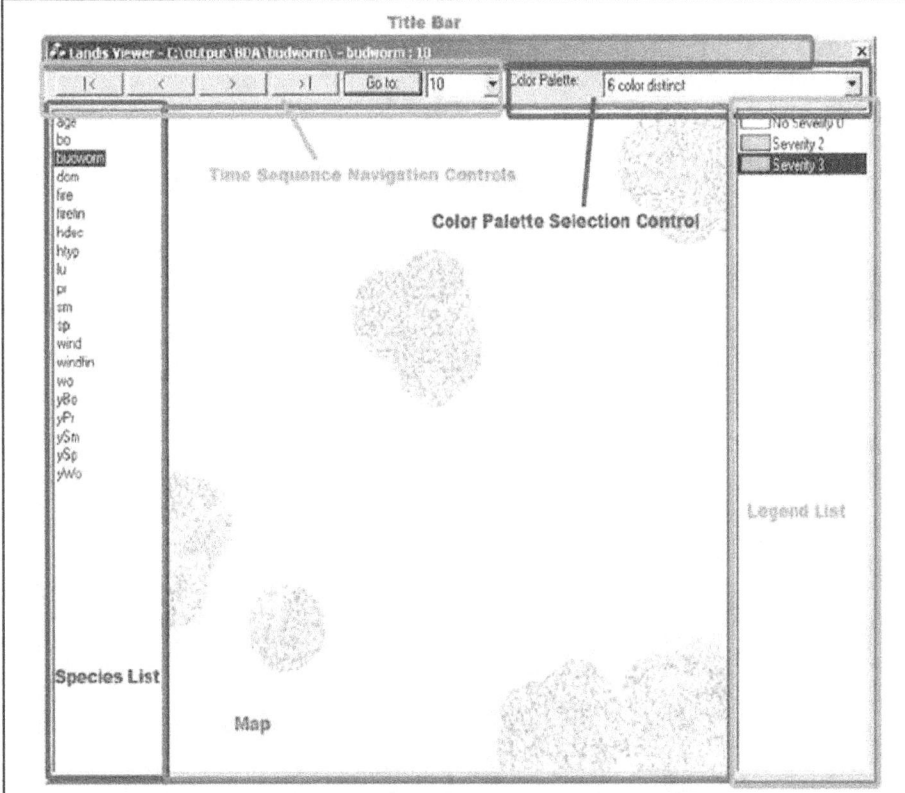

Figure 15. The main user interface of LANDIS Viewer.

Users may choose to display the first, the last, the previous, and the next map in a time sequence by clicking the corresponding buttons. Moreover, users may also display any map they want by inputting the number in the time sequence or selecting the number from the list. In addition, the input control has an input assistant, so that when a number is entered that does not exist in the time sequence, the input control will automatically select the nearest number and display the corresponding map.

The color palette selection control is used to select the color table to draw the map. There are four predefined color tables. They are "6 color distinct," "6 color continuous," "48 color continuous," and "256 color continuous." Users may also choose to use the color table stored in the trailer file if the trailer file corresponding to the gis map file exists.

The species list stores all species and disturbance names in the LANDIS output directory and enables users to choose which species and disturbances will be shown.

The map display shows the currently selected map rendered using the color table specified by the user. The legend list shows the legends for the current map. Only the colors used in the map are shown in the legend list.

These components are not visible at all times. They may be disabled or hidden in some situations. Furthermore, the layout of the user interface may be changed in some situations. For example, time sequence navigation controls may be disabled when a species or disturbance that is currently shown only has a single file. And the navigation controls will be enabled again when a species or disturbance that has a time sequence is chosen.

19.3 How To Use

LANDIS Viewer can be run with or without command line parameters.

When LANDIS Viewer runs without command line parameters, a dialog is shown for selecting a map or a directory to be displayed. The initial color palette is also chosen at this time. Then the main user interface is presented to show the map files.

When it runs with command line parameters, LANDIS Viewer gets the file or directory name and the initial color palette from command line parameters instead of extracting the name and color palette from the dialog. LANDIS Viewer skips the first step, which is showing a dialog to select file/directory name and color palette, and displays the map file/files specified in command line.

LANDIS Viewer can work in two modes: directory mode when a LANDIS output directory is loaded, and file mode when a gis map is loaded.

In directory mode, all of the six user interface components are shown. LANDIS Viewer analyzes the file names under the specified directory, extracts the species/disturbance names, and then fills these names into the species list component. The viewer also extracts the number of years in time sequence and fills the numbers into the time sequence navigation controls component. Therefore, no matter what time step was used in the LANDIS system, LANDIS Viewer can find the right time step and navigate the time sequence correctly. After these procedures are done, the species/disturbance name and the number in the time sequence can be selected to show the map. The legend information will be loaded from the trailer file and shown in the legend list component when the map is loaded.

In file mode, the procedure is quite simple. Species list and time sequence navigation controls are hidden, and legend list will be hidden if there is no trailer file with the map file. The map file specified in the dialog or command line parameter is loaded and shown on the map component using the color palette selected by the user.

19.4 Key Features of LANDIS Viewer

19.4.1 Accept maps of any size

LANDIS Viewer accepts maps of any size, but when the map size is larger than the size of physical memory, it will slow system response time. The user interface of LANDIS Viewer automatically resizes to fit the size of map. If the map size is too large to be shown in one screen, the user interface will be shown as the size of screen and the horizontal/vertical scrolling bar will be shown to scroll the map. The user can also choose to proportionally scale the viewing size by specifying 1/16, 1/8, 1/4, 1/2, 2, 4, 8, and 16 times the original map size.

Important note: In directory mode, all files under the directory are assumed by LANDIS Viewer to have the same map size. LANDIS Viewer only resizes itself when starting up.

19.4.2 Accept both 8-bit and 16-bit maps

LANDIS Viewer accepts maps both 8-bit and 16-bit maps. Since human eyes cannot distinguish more than 256 colors, the viewer uses an index-based color system that only supports 256 colors to draw the map. Therefore, the 16-bit maps must be projected to the 256 color space. The method to project the color space from 16-bit to 8-bit is to classify the values with the same lower 8 bits into one group, so all values in the 16-bit are divided into 256 groups, and each group is assigned one color.

19.4.3 Support command line parameters

LANDIS Viewer accepts command line parameters; thus, the viewer can be called from other programs to show maps specified in command line parameters. The command line parameter format is a file/directory name string followed by a number with value from 0 to 4 that indicates the initial color palette. The file/directory name can be enclosed with quote symbol if it contains a blank space character. LANDIS Viewer decides whether the name is a file name or a directory name and runs in the correct mode. For the number of initial color palette, values 0 to 3 indicate the use of one of the three predefined color palettes, "6 color distinct," "6 color continuous," "48 color continuous," and "256 color continuous" correspondingly. Value 4 causes LANDIS Viewer to use the color palette stored in the trailer file. The examples of command line parameters are as follows:

> LV.exe c:\output 0
>
> > LANDIS Viewer shows all maps in c:\output using "6 color distinct" color palette.
>
> LV.exe "c:\output\age0.gis" 4
>
> > LANDIS Viewer shows the map c:\output\age0.gis using the color palette stored in trailer file c:\output\age0.trl.

19 OUTPUT VIEWER

19.4.4 Species list and time sequence navigation

LANDIS output maps are a pair of files composed of a map file with extension name "*.gis" and a trailer file with extension name "*.trl." These maps can be classified to two types, single maps and time sequence maps. The file name for single maps is formed by "species/disturbances name" + "extension name." And the file name for time sequence maps is formed by "species/disturbances name" + "number of time sequence" + "extension name." For instance, file firefin.gis is the map file for cumulative fire damage assessment, which is a single map file; and file age0.gis is the map file of age sequence at year 0, which is a map file in a time sequence.

In directory mode, LANDIS Viewer assumes all of the time sequence results have the same time step. LANDIS Viewer arranges files by species/disturbances and time sequence and shows Species List and Time Sequence Navigation Controls to let users select a file. LANDIS Viewer puts all species/disturbances names into the Species List. When users choose a single map species, the time sequence navigation controls are disabled. And when users choose a time sequence map species, these navigation controls are enabled. Users can iterate the time sequence results by using navigation controls.

19.4.5 Multiple instances of the viewer

LANDIS Viewer supports multi-instances. Users can open as many LANDIS Viewer windows as they need under the limitation of the operation system. These windows won't interrupt each other in either file mode or directory mode.

20. LANDIS SUBSIDIARY PROGRAMS

20.1 IAN-Raster Image Analysis Software Program

IAN generates reports from the statistical analysis of raster images. It is programmed in the open source scripting language Ruby, enabling technically savvy users and the developers to easily extend the program. The existing framework is designed to easily support additional metrics, reports, image file formats, options, and units. The flexible architecture of IAN streamlines the process of new releases. IAN runs on all 32-bit Windows platforms. It comes with two user interfaces-a user friendly windowing user interface (IAN) and a command line user interface (IANC) for console and programmatic access. If you have any questions about IAN, send them to ian-mail@mailplus.wisc.edu.

20.2 Map Converter

Mapconvert.exe is a stand-alone program to convert maps among text format, ERDAS GIS 7.4 8-bit, and ERDAS GIS 7.4 16-bit. To run the program type

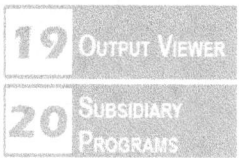

> **mapconvert**
>
> **Enter input file:** *enter input file here*
>
> **Enter format 1) ASCII, 2) 8-bit, 3) 16-bit:** *1 or 2 or 3*
>
> **Enter output file:** *enter output file here*
>
> **Enter format 1) ASCII, 2) 8-bit, 3) 16-bit:** *1 or 2 or 3*

Or you can enter all the information at one time, e.g.,

> **mapconvert** *[input file name] [format 1|2|3] [output file name]*
> *[format 1|2|3]*

20.3 GIS2Grid

GIS2Grid is a utility that generates three script files used for converting LANDIS output (or any folder where there are .gis files) into ascii files, converting such ascii files into grid files, and assisting Fragstats to read such grid files for further analysis, respectively.

GIS2Grid package includes two exe files: gis2grid.exe and Mapconvert.exe. Mapconvert.exe is a stand-alone program used for converting gis files into ASCII files or vice versa. Gis2grid.exe can generate the three script files.

Here are the instructions for using it:

1) When you click gis2grid.exe, a dialog window pops up. You need to tell the program where mapconvert.exe is located in your local computer. Click "open the mapconvertor" button and select the file from the dialog (fig. 16).

2) Now, tell the program which folder contains the LANDIS output (or any folder that contains gis files). Click "Open a file from the LANDIS output folder" button. You can select any file under the folder (fig. 17).

3) Specify the folder where you want to save your converted ASCII and grid files (fig. 18).

4) When you finish the above steps, click "OK" to run it. The program will generate three script files and save them in the selected folder (fig. 19).

5) Convert GIS files into ASCII files. Just click the first script files called "ascii.bat." It will run mapconvert.exe in the batch mode (fig. 5). The converted ASCII files will be saved in the folder "converted folder\ascii\" (fig. 20).

6) Now you can invoke ArcToolbox (Tucker 2000) to convert ASCII files to raster (grid) files. You need to run "ASCII to Grid" in batch mode (fig. 21).

7) When the "ASCII to Grid" tool reads the "grid.aml" file that was generated from this utility (fig. 7), it will convert all ASCII files into grids under the folder: "converted folder\grid\" (fig. 22).

8) If you have the Windows version of FRAGSTATS (which can be downloaded from http://www.umass.edu/landeco/research/fragstats/ fragstats.html), you can let FRAGSTATS read the batch file "frag.fbt" to read all converted grids into FRAGSTATS for further analysis (fig. 23).

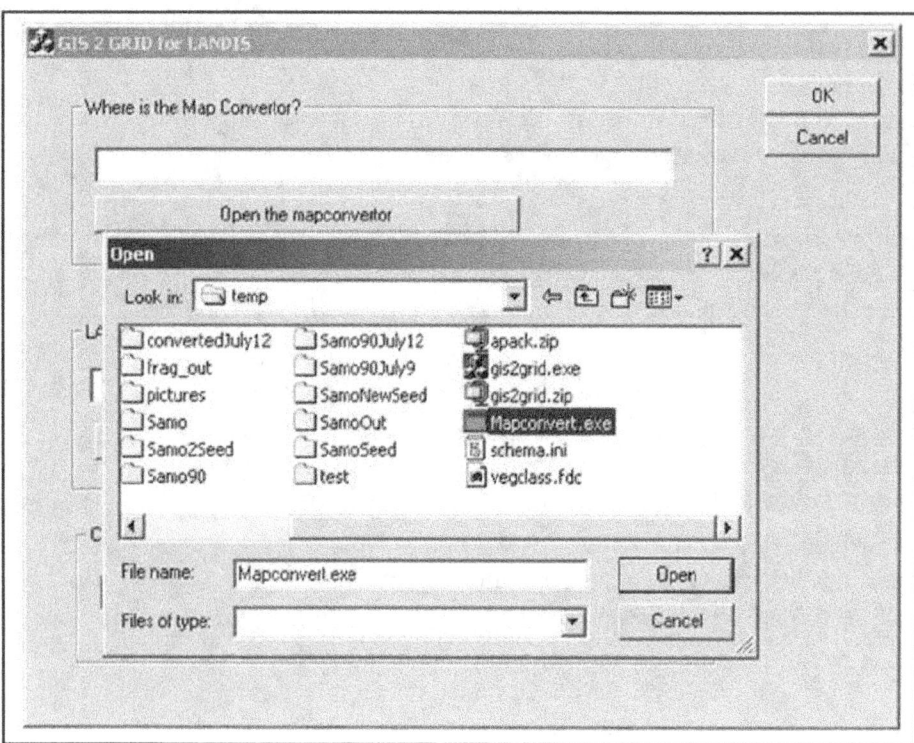

Figure 16. Window interface of the mapconvert program.

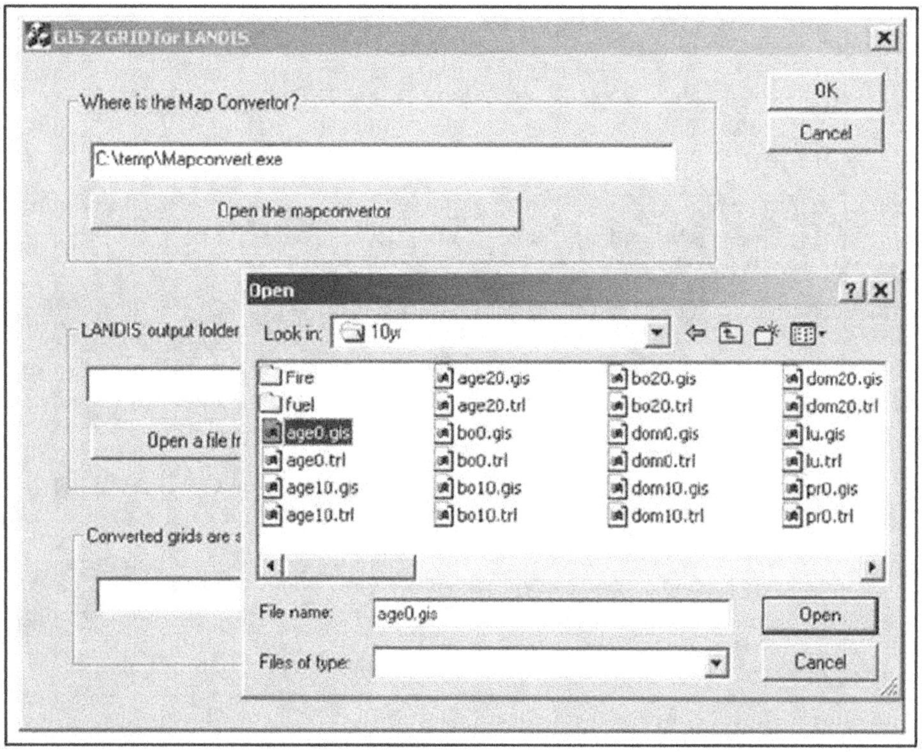

Figure 17. Choose LANDIS output folder using the mapconvert program.

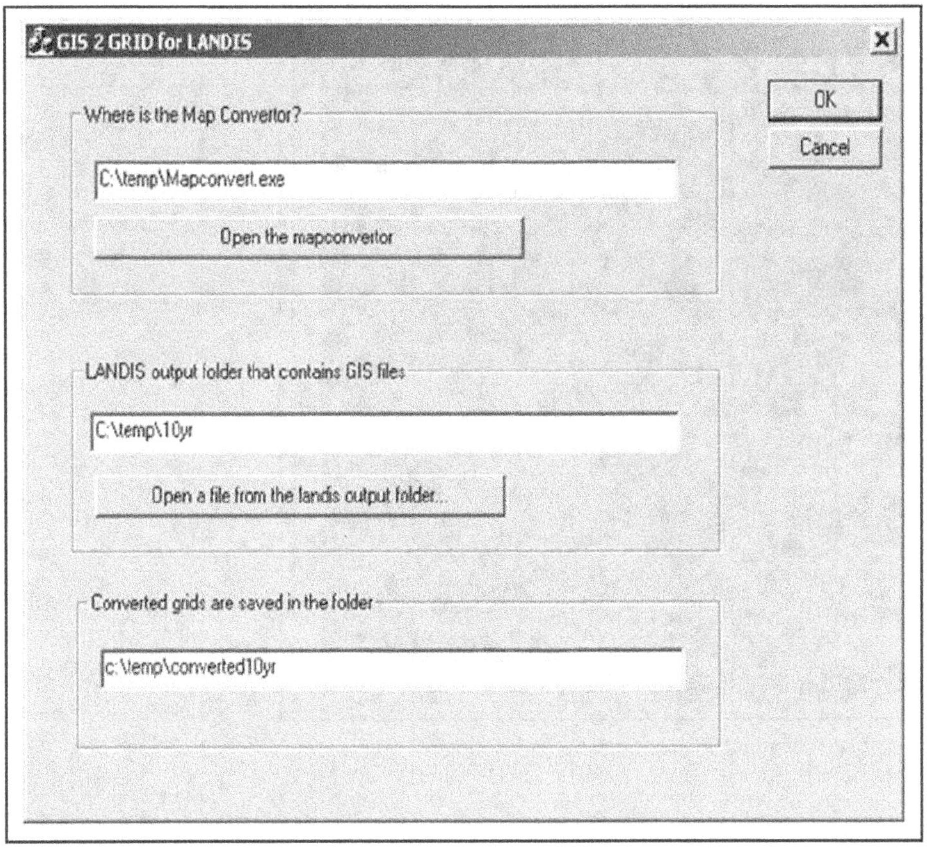

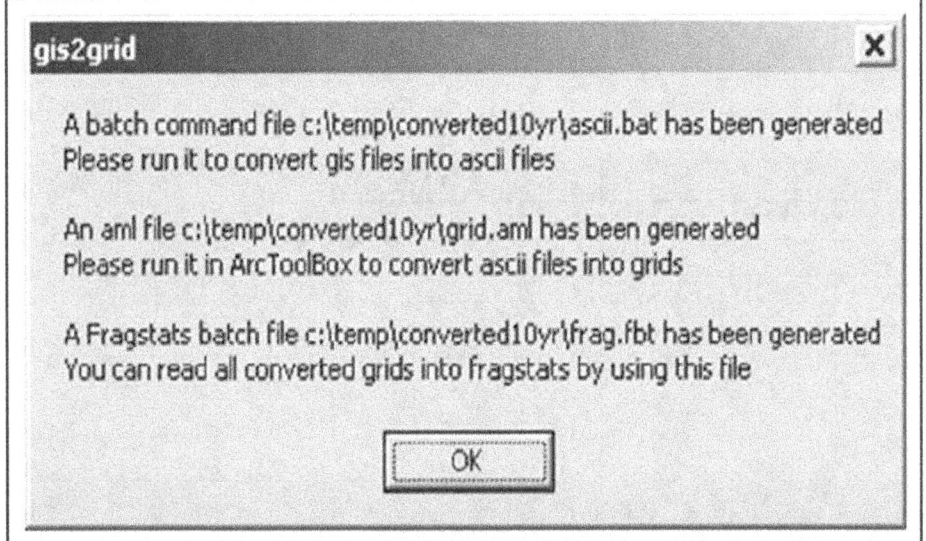

Figure 18. Choose the converted folder.

Figure 19. The pop-up window tells you where you can find the three script files.

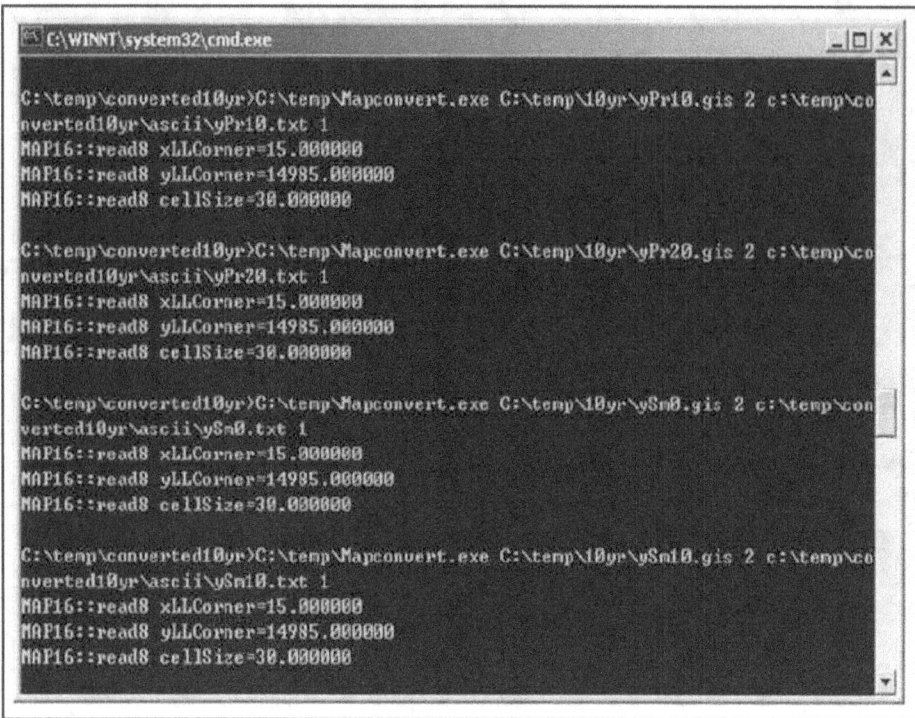

Figure 20. Mapconvert.exe is now converting GIS files into ASCII files.

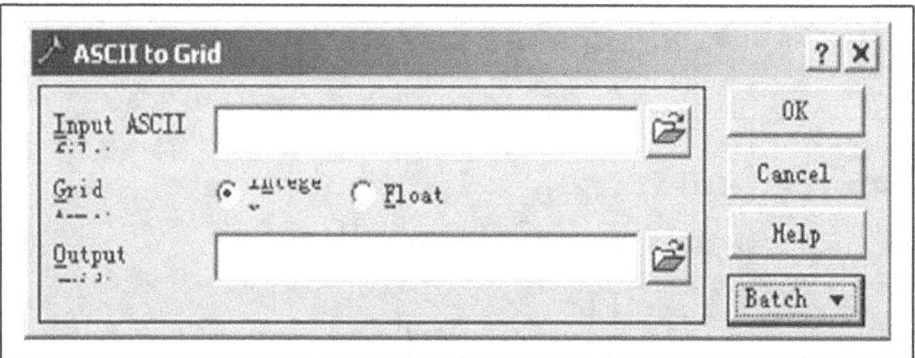

Figure 21. Converting ASCII to Grid using ArcToolbox.

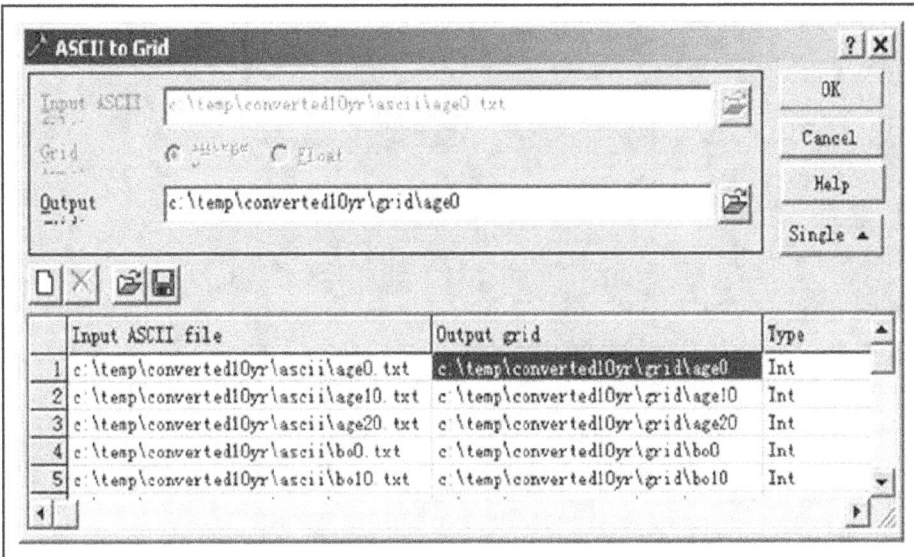

Figure 22. Reading in the "grid.aml" file.

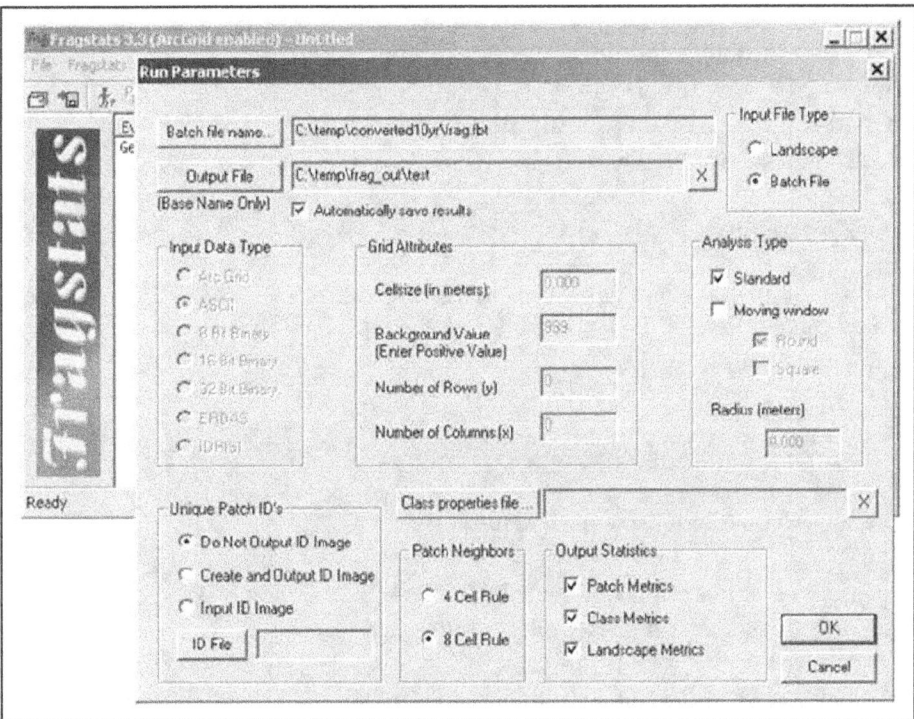

Figure 23. FRAGSTATS can read frag.fbt.

21.   QUICK EVALUATION OF RESULTS

There are no strict criteria for evaluating LANDIS results since LANDIS is a stochastic model driven by millions of random numbers. We recommend that users read the Major References regarding a specific discussion. Still, there are three aspects we check when examining LANDIS results.

21.1 Mean Disturbance Sizes

If a natural disturbance is turned on, you can calculate the means for Damage Size from the LANDIS disturbance log file. It is usually called WIND.LOG or FIRE.LOG in the default output directory.

For wind disturbance, compare the mean disturbance size summarized from WIND.LOG with respective mean disturbance size set for wind in the LANDIS disturbance file. If the simulated value differs significantly, it implies that the wind disturbance size curve may not represent the correct wind disturbance size distribution for the simulated area. Adjust the corresponding parameters in the parameter file and conduct another run.

For fire disturbance, compare mean disturbance sizes summarized for each land type in FIRE.LOG with the specific mean disturbance sizes set for each land type in the land type attribute input file. Sometimes it can be hard to determine if the run is valid, since simulated mean fire disturbance sizes match well on certain land types but not on others. A t-test is suggested to check the significance of differences for such cases. If there is a significant difference at the 85 percent level, we suggest that the fire disturbance size curve may not represent the correct fire disturbance size distribution of the simulated area. Adjust the corresponding parameters in the parameter file and conduct another run.

21.2 Mean Disturbance Return Intervals

Mean disturbance return interval can be considered as the expected (or average) time required to disturb an area equal in size to the study area. This can also be extracted from disturbance log files.

For wind disturbance, compare the simulated total disturbance size with the expected total disturbance size. The latter can be calculated as follows:

$$\text{Expected total disturbance size} = \text{Area} * \text{Years} / \text{meanReturn}$$

where Area is the total study area, Years is the final simulated year, and meanReturn is the mean wind disturbance return interval. If the simulated total disturbance size does not match the expected total disturbance size, the wind disturbance probability curve may not be correct for the simulation. Adjust the corresponding parameters in the parameter file and conduct another run.

For fire disturbance, compare the simulated total disturbance sizes summarized for each land type with the expected total disturbance sizes calculated for each land type using the above formula. As in the evaluation for mean disturbance size discussed earlier, a t-test may be used to check for significant differences. If there is a significant difference at the 85 percent level, we suggest that the fire disturbance probability curve may not represent the correct fire probability of the simulated area. Adjust the corresponding parameters in the parameter file and conduct another run.

21 EVALUATION OF RESULTS

22.   TROUBLESHOOTING

Here are solutions to some common problems when running LANDIS. For other technical problems contact Hong S. He at the address provided on page ii.

22.1 Missing Dlls

This error indicates that Msvcrt.dll or Mfc42.dll is not found in any subdirectory specified in the PATH environmental variable. Add the subdirectory where these files reside to your PATH.

22.2 Program Terminated with an Error Message Displayed

Usually the error message explains the reason why the program was terminated. Follow the instructions in Preparing Files for a LANDIS Run. If the error message is unclear, check your parameter input file and all the files required. The following are the most common errors when conducting a LANDIS run:

1) Each '#' has a matching '#' in all comments.

2) Nonactive land types must be one these types: empty, water, lowland, wetland, bog, nonforest. Land type names are case sensitive.

3) The upper level of specified output directory does not exist (look for typos).

4) The species listed in the land type file do not match the species listed in the species file.

5) The species listed in the map attribute file do not match the species listed in the species file.

6) Some index names specified in the map index file do not have the corresponding RCS files defined. Reclassification will not occur for that specific type.

7) The RCS file contains a species name that does not match the name in the species file.

8) The format of one or more RCS files is not correct.

9) Some age index names specified in the age index files do not have the corresponding AGE files defined.

10) Some species names in an AGE file do not match the species names in the species file.

22.3 Program Hung

After LANDIS is started, it should not take long before signs of LANDIS processing appears on the screen. If nothing appears on the screen except for the command you typed, the program might be allocating memory. If you hear the hard disk working, the program is probably allocating virtual memory. If you are waiting more than a few minutes (depending on your computer), the program is probably hung. Make sure that the parameter file and all other required files were created correctly.

22.4 Abnormal Program Termination

This message usually means there is not enough virtual memory available on your machine. It usually happens at the very beginning of a LANDIS run. To alleviate the problem you can:

1) Increase virtual memory.
2) Run your simulation on a smaller area or at a coarser resolution.
3) Decrease the total number of species or the total number of land types in your simulation.

22.5 Out of Memory

This can happen during processing. Occasionally LANDIS needs to allocate memory during a run. To alleviate the problem see Abnormal Program Termination.

22.6 Out of Disk Space

There is not enough space left on your hard drive to complete your simulation. Do one or more of the following:

1) Reorganize your reclassification file so that each map contains more information.
2) Decrease the number of reclassification methods in the map index file to output fewer maps.
3) Change the frequency.out file to decrease output intervals.

22.7 Program is Very Slow

1) You are running a simulation on a very large map.
2) The species file contains many species that are not present in your work area; delete unnecessary species definitions.
3) The seeding routine chosen is very slow. Choose a different one.
4) Inactive land types are treated as active land types. Check land type names.

22.8 Results and Parameters Do Not Match

LANDIS is a random number driven stochastic model. There will never be a perfect match for disturbance size and mean return interval between the LANDIS input files and the LANDIS output files. The equations generating disturbance frequencies and disturbance sizes rely on random number generation and empirical coefficients. These equations can lead to stable matches when total simulation years reach several thousands.

22.9 LANDIS Users Forum

LANDIS 4.0 update and bug fixing will be posted on www.snr.missouri/ LANDIS. LANDIS Users Forum provides free access for LANDIS users to share news and various issues in using LANDIS. The Web address is www.snr.missouri/ LANDIS.

22.10 Acknowledgments

We would like to thank John Waldron, Pat Zollner, and many others who helped improve this users guide.

23. REFERENCES

Agee, J.; Huff, M. 1987. Fuel succession in a western hemlock/Douglas-fir forest. Canadian Journal of Forest Research. 17: 697-704.

Armour, C. D.; Bunting, S. C.; Neuenschwander, L. F. 1984. Fire intensity effects on the understory in ponderosa pine forests. Journal of Range Management. 37: 44-49.

Baker, W. L.; Egbert, S. L.; Frazier, G. F. 1991. A spatial model for studying the effects of climatic change on the structure of landscapes subject to large disturbances. Ecological Modelling. 56: 109-125.

Bergeron, C. H. Y.; Flannigan, M. D. 2000. Coarse woody debris in the southeastern Canadian boreal forest: composition and load variations in relation to stand replacement. Canadian Journal of Forest Research. 30: 674-687.

Botkin, D. B.; Janak, J. G.; Wallis, J. R., 1972. Some ecological consequences of a computer model of forest growth. Journal of Ecology. 60: 849-872.

Botkin, D. B., 1993. Forest dynamics: an ecological model. Oxford, UK: Oxford University Press: 101-138.

Brose, P.; Wade, D. 2002. Potential fire behavior in pine flatwood forests following three different fuel reduction techniques. Forest Ecology and Management. 163: 71-84.

Brown, J. K.; See, T. E. 1981. Downed dead woody fuel and biomass in the northern Rocky Mountains. Gen. Tech. Rep. INT-117. Ogden, UT: U.S. Department of Agriculture, Forest Service, Intermountain Forest and Range Experiment Station: 1-47.

Brown, J. K.; Oberheu, R. D.; Johnston, C. M. 1982. Handbook for inventory surface fuels and biomass in the interior west. Gen. Tech. Rep. INT-129. Ogden, UT: U.S. Department of Agriculture, Forest Service, Intermountain Forest and Range Experiment Station: 1-48.

Cappuccino, N.; Lavertu, D.; Bergeron, Y.; Regniere, J. 1998. Spruce budworm impact, abundance and parasitism rate in a patchy landscape. Oecologia. 114: 236-242.

Clarke, D. C.; Brass, J. A.; Riggan, P. J. 1994. A cellular automaton model of wildfire propagation and extinction. Photogrammetry Engineering and Remote Sensing. 60: 1335-1367.

Foster J. R.; Lang, G. E. 1982. Decomposition of red spruce and balsam fir boles in the White Mountains of New Hampshire. Canadian Journal of Forest Research. 12: 617-626.

Gardner, R. H. 1999. RULE: map generation and spatial analysis program. In: Landscape ecological analysis: issues and applications. New York, NY: Springer-Verlag: 280-303.

Gardner, R. H.; Romme, W. H.; Turner, M. G. 1999. Effects of scale-dependent processes on predicting patterns of forest fires. In: Mladenoff D.J.; Baker W. L., eds. Advances in spatial modeling of forest landscape change: approaches and applications. Cambridge, UK: Cambridge University Press: 163-185

Grier, C. C.; Logan, R. S. 1977. Old-growth Pseudotsuga menziesii communities of a western Oregon watershed: biomass distribution and production budgets. Ecological Monograph. 47: 373-400.

Gustafson, E. J.; Shifley, S. R.; Mladenoff, D. J.; et al. 2000. Spatial simulation of forest succession and harvesting using LANDIS. Canadian Journal of Forest Research. 30: 32-43.

Gustafson, E. J.; Zollner, P. A.; Sturtevant, B. R.; et al. 2004. Influence of forest management alternatives and land type on susceptibility to fire in northern Wisconsin, USA. Landscape Ecology. 19: 327-341.

Hale, C. M.; Pastor, J. 1998. Nitrogen content, decay rates and decompositional dynamics of hollow versus solid hardwood logs in hardwood forests of Minnesota, USA. Canadian Journal of Forest Research. 28: 1276-1285.

Hardy, C. C.; Schmidt, K. M.; Menakis, J. M.; Samson, N. R. 2001. Spatial data for national forest planning and fuel management. International Journal of Wildland Fire 10: 353-372.

Hargrove, W. W.; Gardner, R. H.; Turner, M. G.; et al. 2000. Simulating fire patterns in heterogeneous landscapes. Ecological Modelling. 135: 243-263.

Harmon, M. E.; Franklin, J. F.; Swanson, F. J.; et al. 1986. Ecology of coarse woody debris in temperate ecosystems. Advanced Ecological Research. 15: 133-302.

He, H. S.; Mladenoff, D. J. 1999a. Spatially explicit and stochastic simulation of forest landscape fire disturbance and succession. Ecology. 80: 81-99.

He, H. S.; Mladenoff, D. J. 1999b. Effects of seed dispersal in the simulation of long-term forest landscape change. Ecosystems. 2: 308-319.

He, H. S.; Larsen, D. R.; Mladenoff, D. J. 2002. Exploring component based approaches in forest landscape modeling. Environmental Modelling and Software. 17: 519-529.

He, H. S.; Mladenoff, D. J.; Boeder, J. 1999a. An object-oriented forest landscape model and its representation of tree species. Ecological Modelling. 119: 1-19.

He, H. S.; Mladenoff, D. J.; Crow, T. R. 1999b. Linking an ecosystem model and a landscape model to study individual species response to climate change. Ecological Modelling. 112: 213-233.

He, H. S.; Mladenoff, D. J.; Radeloff, V. C.; Crow, T. R. 1998. Integration of GIS data and classified satellite imagery for regional forest assessment. Ecological Applications. 8: 1072-1083.

He, H. S.; Shang Z. B.; Crow, T. R.; et al. 2004. Simulating forest fuel and fire risk dynamics across landscapes-LANDIS fuel module design. Ecological Modelling. 180: 135-151.

Johnson, E. A. 1992. Fire and vegetation dynamics: studies from the North American boreal forest. Cambridge, UK: Cambridge University Press.

Johnson, E. A.; Fryer, G. I.; Heathcott, M. J. 1990. The influence of man and climate on frequency of fire in the interior wet belt forest, British Columbia. Journal of Ecology. 78: 403-412.

Lambert, R. L.; Lang, G. E.; Reiners, W. A. 1980. Loss of mass and chemical change in decaying boles of a subalpine balsam fir forest. Ecology. 61: 1460-1473.

Lang, C. E.; Forman, R. T. T. 1978. Detritus dynamics in a mature oak forest: Hutcheson Memorial Forest, New Jersey. Ecology. 57: 580-595.

Li, C. 2001. Fire disturbance patterns and forest age structure. Natural Resource Modeling. 14: 495-521.

Li, C. 2000. Reconstruction of natural fire regimes through ecological modelling. Ecological Modelling. 134: 129-144.

Li, W.; He, H. S. 2004. LANDIS 4.0 programming technical report. Columbia, MO: School of Natural Resources, University of Missouri-Columbia. 29 p.

MacMillan, P. C. 1988. Decomposition of coarse woody debris in an old-growth Indiana forest. Canadian Journal of Forest Research. 18: 1353-1362.

Mladenoff, D. J. 2004. LANDIS and forest landscape models. Ecological Modelling. 180: 7-19.

Mladenoff, D. J.; He, H. S. 1999. Design and behavior of LANDIS, an object-oriented model of forest landscape disturbance and succession. In: Mladenoff, D. J.; Baker, W. L., eds. Advances in spatial modeling of forest landscape change: approaches and applications. Cambridge, UK: Cambridge University Press:163-185.

Mladenoff, J. D.; Host, G. E.; Boeder, J.; Crow, T. R. 1996. LANDIS: a spatial model of forest landscape disturbance succession, and management. In: Goodchild, M. F.; et al. eds. GIS and environmental modeling: progress and research issues. Fort Collins, CO: GIS World Inc.

Orr, M. J. L. 1996. Introduction to radial basis function networks. http://www.anc.ed.ac/uk/mjo/intro/intro.html.

23 REFERENCES

Pastor, J.; Post, W. M. 1985. Development of a linked forest productivity-soil process model. Oak Ridge, TN: Oak Ridge National Laboratory: 162.

Pickett, S. T. A.; Thompson, J. N. 1978. Patch dynamics and the design of nature reserves. Biological Conservation. 13: 27-47.

Pickett, S. T. A.; White, P. S. 1985. The ecology of natural disturbance and patch dynamics. New York, NY: Academic Press.

Pickett, S. T. A.; Amesto, J. J.; Collins, S. L. 1989. The ecological concept of disturbance and its expression at various hierarchical levels. Oikos. 54: 129-136.

Radeloff, V.C.; Mladenoff, D.J.; Boyce, M.S. 2000. The changing relation of landscape patterns and jack pine budworm populations during an outbreak. Oikos. 90: 417-430.

Roberts, D. W. 1996. Modeling forest dynamics with vital attributes and fuzzy systems theory. Ecological Modelling. 90: 161-173.

Shang, Z. B.; He, H. S.; Crow, T. R.; Shifley, S. R. 2004. Fuel load reductions and fire risk in central hardwood forests of the United States: a spatial simulation study. Ecological Modelling. 180: 89-102.

Shugart, H. H., 1984. A theory of forest dynamics. New York, NY: Springer-Verlag: 48-67.

Shugart, H. H., 1997. Terrestrial ecosystems in changing environments -Cambridge studies in ecology. Cambridge, UK: Cambridge University Press: 343-380.

Spetich, M. A.; Shifley, S. R.; Parker, G. R., 1999. Regional distribution and dynamics of coarse woody debris in midwestern old-growth forests. Forest Science. 45: 302-313.

Spies, T. A.; Franklin, J. F.; Thomas, T. B. 1988. Coarse woody debris in Douglas-fir forests of western Oregon and Washington. Ecology. 69: 1698-1702.

Sturtevant, B. R.; Bissonette, J. A.; Long, J. N.; Roberts, D. W. 1997. Coarse woody debris as a function of age, stand structure, and disturbance in boreal Newfoundland. Ecological Applications. 7: 702-712.

Sturtevant, B. R.; Gustafson, E. J.; Li, W.; He, H. S. 2004. Modeling biological disturbances in LANDIS: a module description and demonstration using spruce budworm. Ecological Modelling. 180: 153-174.

Turner, M. G.; Romme, W. H.; Gardner, R. H. 1994. Landscape disturbance models and the long-term dynamics of natural areas. Natural Areas Journal. 14: 3-11.

Urban, D. L.; Harmon, M. E.; Halpern, C. B. 1993. Potential response of Pacific Northwestern forests to climatic change, effects of stand age and initial composition. Climatic Change. 23: 247-266.

Wimberley, M. C.; Spies, T. A.; Long, C. J.; Whitlock, C. 2000. Simulating historical variability in the amount of old forests in the Oregon Coast Range. Conservation Biology. 14: 167-180.

Yang, J.; He, H. S.; Gustafson, E. J. 2004. A hierarchical statistical approach to simulate the temporal patterns of forest fire disturbance in LANDIS model. Ecological Modelling. 180: 119-133.

www.ingramcontent.com/pod-product-compliance
Lightning Source LLC
Chambersburg PA
CBHW080313290526
45790CB00005B/2019